GCSE

SKILLS

SPOKEN LANGUAGE STUDY

Ellie Aslin
Dan Clayton
Julia Glozier
Series Editor: Imelda Pilgrim

Nelson Thornes

D0178930

Published in 2013 by:
Nelson Thornes Ltd
Delta Place
27 Bath Road
CHELTENHAM
GL53 7TH
United Kingdom

13 14 15 16 17 / 10 9 8 7 6 5 4 3 2 1

A catalogue record for this book is available from the British Library

ISBN 978 1 4085 1914 1

Page make-up and illustrations by Fakenham Prepress Solutions
Illustrations by Bridget Dowty, Elisabeth Eudes-Pascal and Brett Hudson
of GCI Illustration
Printed in China by 1010 Printing International Ltd

Acknowledgements

Images p6, Britain's Got Talent poster: Robert Gray/Alamy; p7, interview in a restaurant: Deklofenak/
iStockphoto; p9, Jonas Brothers: London Red Carpet/Alamy; p16, Tulisa: Ken McKay/Thames/Rex Features;
p18, corner shop: © By Ian Miles-Flashpoint Pictures/Alamy; p20, teenager on phone: leminuit/iStockphoto;
p24, Jason Cundy: Piers Allardyce/Rex Features; p27, Job interview: MichaelDeLeon/iStockphoto; p29,
Oleanna: Photostage; p30, *Oleanna*: Photostage; p33, discussing plans: kali9/iStockphoto; p34, Professor
Brian Cox: Getty Images; p35, boy with kestrel: Fotolia; p37, Graffiti: Fotolia; p37, Plan B: WireImage/
Getty Images; p40, young man and a motorcycle: Frank Bez Getty Images; p48, ice cream seller: © Kumar
Sriskandan/Alamy; p53, protest: Paul Grover/Rex Features; p57, young man at computer: uniquely india/
Getty Images; p59, Michelle Obama: © Ken Cedeno/Corbis; p61, Bill Clinton: © Ron Sachs/CNP/Corbis;
p66, Cavendish in Tour de Angleterre: © Rob Pinney/Demotix/Corbis; p72, The Inbetweeners: © Photos 12/
Alamy; p77, Channel 4 News: © Mark Makela/Corbis; p81, Death of a Salesman: © AF archive/Alamy; p85,
David Tennant: Getty Images; p90, Emma Thompson: WireImage/Getty Images.

Contents

Spoken language skills for GCSE iv

1 Non-fluency features: Making it up as you go along 1

2 Interaction and the structure of talk: Following the rules 16

3 Lexis: The words we use 32

4 Grammar and structure: Stories, texts and tweets 45

5 Planned and unplanned speech: The right words at the right time 58

6 Implied meanings: Why don't you say what you mean? 72

7 Attitudes to spoken language: 'It ain't what you say, it's the way that
  you say it' 85

  Glossary 91

Spoken language skills for GCSE

This book has been written to introduce you to the study of spoken language which will form part of your English Language GCSE. The study of spoken language has been a compulsory part of GCSE specifications since 2010 and this topic offers you a chance to look at forms of language you might never have studied in detail.

The activities in this book have been designed to help you develop your knowledge of spoken language and build your skills so that you can analyse a person's speech effectively. More specifically, this book aims to:

- help you understand the way that spoken language differs from other forms of language
- develop your awareness of some of the typical features of spoken language
- encourage you to explore the different factors that influence how people speak, interact and respond to one another
- give you advice about how to approach analysing examples of spoken language.

The student book is divided into seven units, which each focus on a different aspect of spoken language. You will find that there are many links between units, so the knowledge and skills you gain in one unit might come in useful in another.

Each unit contains an annotated example demonstrating how you can go about analysing the details of spoken language. The glossary of keywords provides you with the vocabulary you need to be able to talk about spoken language precisely.

The examples of spoken language that have been included in this book come from a variety of situations. There are conversations between family and friends, interactions in schools and interviews, speech transcribed from radio and TV, as well as scripted forms such as play scripts and speeches.

The carefully structured range of activities that accompany these examples will help to build your understanding gradually and give you opportunities to develop key skills in speaking and listening, reading and writing.

Learning to read transcriptions

Lots of the examples of spoken language included in this book are real-life examples that have been transcribed (written down) so that you can analyse

them. When spoken language is transcribed, it is important that every little detail is included in the transcript, even the things that seem like mistakes.

You will notice that the transcriptions of spoken language look different to most written forms of text. There are several ways to present and lay out a transcription. In this book the transcripts do not contain punctuation marks such as commas, full stops, question marks and exclamation marks.

You will also notice that the transcripts contain symbols that you might never have seen before. The key explains what some of these symbols mean.

Key

// This marking will be seen where two people speak at the same time. You can tell which words have overlapped because // marks the beginning and end of the overlap. The lines are usually arranged on top of each other too, to make it really clear that they overlap.

= This mark can be seen at the end of one unit of speech and the beginning of the next one. It signals that there is no gap between the two speakers talking, that one person's speech latches on to the next.

(.) This is a very short pause of less than a second.

(1) This shows a longer pause. The number tells you how many seconds the pause lasts.

Words in **bold** signal that the speaker has used his or her voice to put extra emphasis on the word, saying it slightly louder or with more force.

Getting the most out of this book

We also hope that you are able to relate the examples of spoken language we have selected to your own experiences. You might like to use your new understanding of spoken language to analyse your own speech and to think about the impact it might have on the people you speak to. Spoken language is all around you, so if you want to extend your studies, there are plenty of sources of spoken language out there. Try transcribing and analysing some of your own!

Non-fluency features: Making it up as you go along

Most forms of spoken language used on a day-to-day basis are spontaneous and unplanned. We react to the situations we are faced with, we think quickly and we try to respond in an appropriate way. Of course, this is easier said than done, and it is no surprise that sometimes we make mistakes in our speech, get our words muddled up and struggle to find the right expression, or just forget what we were going to say!

As you work through this book, you will notice that the **transcripts** of spoken language include every little detail of the person's speech, such as:

- tiny pauses and other types of hesitation;
- the repetition of words and phrases;
- people speaking at the same time.

These are called non-fluency features. In this unit you will look at several kinds of non-fluency features which can disrupt the smooth flow of speech and you will be asked to think about where, when, how and why these features become part of our spoken language.

An annotated example

In the following transcript 22-year-old James is being interviewed by a researcher about his hobbies and pastimes. The interviewer wants to gather as much information as possible from James but she wants him to be relaxed so that he is more willing to talk to her. There are lots of non-fluency features present because of the informal and mostly spontaneous nature of the interaction.

Key terms

Transcript: words written down exactly as they have been spoken.

Utterance: when someone speaks, we usually refer to each unit of speech as an utterance. This term can be used for very tiny or very long amounts of speech that are said all in one go.

Overlapping: talking at the same time as someone else. This can be marked in a number of ways. In this book we have indicated this by placing // at the beginning and end of the overlap.

Interviewer:	all right (.) erm (.) so what about internet and TV (.) does that take up a lot of your time (1) like spending a lot of time online
James:	I'd say it takes about ninety per cent of my life
Interviewer:	[laughter] //right//
James:	//on Facebook// or the internet
Interviewer:	right Facebook (.) so what do you do when you are on (.) what do you do when you are online

The interviewer wants to get started. Her **utterance** starts slowly, with some pauses in her speech, which may give her a chance to gather her thoughts and formulate her question.

She uses words like 'all right' in order to let James know she is ready to ask another question.

Sometimes **overlapping** occurs. Here, when James pauses in his speech, the interviewer thinks he has finished so begins to talk again, but then James carries on and adds to his last response. As the interviewer wants to hear what he has to say, she gives way and lets him carry on speaking.

The interviewer seems to ask her question, stop, and then ask it again. If you look closely, you see the wording is slightly different. It might be that she was going to ask James what he does on Facebook, but decided against this question because it was too personal or too specific. Instead, she asks him what he does online, which may allow him to talk about a wider range of activities.

We can see James is a bit hesitant and vague in his answers, starting off with some **voiced pauses** and **fillers** that make his answer have less impact.

The interviewer wants to encourage James to keep talking so she sometimes overlaps his speech with comments that support what he is saying.

There are two instances of repetition here: sometimes it is purposeful and sometimes it is accidental. Here, it could be argued that James purposely repeats 'stupid' to emphasise his point. When he repeats 'can't', however, it seems to be more through hesitation. Think carefully about the **context** in order to decide for yourself the reasons behind these details.

Sometimes the speakers echo each other's words. Here James picks up on the word 'YouTube' to show he agrees with what she has suggested. The interviewer does this too, echoing the word 'videos'.

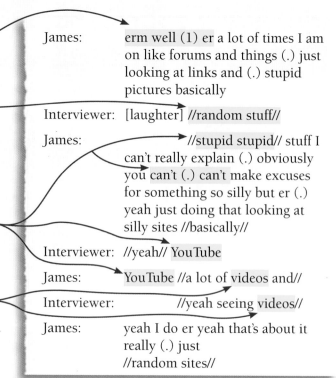

James:	erm well (1) er a lot of times I am on like forums and things (.) just looking at links and (.) stupid pictures basically
Interviewer:	[laughter] //random stuff//
James:	//stupid stupid// stuff I can't really explain (.) obviously you can't (.) can't make excuses for something so silly but er (.) yeah just doing that looking at silly sites //basically//
Interviewer:	//yeah// YouTube
James:	YouTube //a lot of videos and//
Interviewer:	//yeah seeing videos//
James:	yeah I do er yeah that's about it really (.) just //random sites//

Review and reflect

The interview continues and a second person, Hayley, is drawn into the conversation. Look closely at the transcript. What non-fluency features, typical of **spontaneous speech** are present? You could copy out the transcript and label the features.

Interviewer:	//OK// (1) Hayley are you online a lot as well
Hayley:	yes
Interviewer:	(.) what do you do
Hayley:	erm I (.) I have to check my emails about 20 times
Interviewer:	oh yeah oh I am like that [laughter]
Hayley:	an hour erm [laughter] yeah even even when I am at work I try to check my emails erm and also I use it a lot for for research (.) for my course
Interviewer:	oh sure sure
James:	I do that too I'd like to say
Interviewer:	//[laughter]//
Hayley:	//[laughter]//
James:	//I mean I've// got loads it is good for downloading journals and things

Mind the gap

Everyone pauses when they speak; they have to – even if it is just to breathe! In a transcript you will see:

- the pauses in speech marked like this (.), which is a very short pause of less than a second
- or you will see (1), where the number tells you how many seconds the pause lasts.

However, we are not always silent when we pause and there are sounds and words that we use to fill the gaps. 'Er' and 'erm' are just two sounds we make as we pause and think about what to say next. We can call these types of sounds voiced pauses.

Sometimes we use whole words or phrases to fill those gaps. You might be someone, or know someone, who uses the word 'like' a lot in speech. When this word is used in places where it seems to have no meaning, it can be called a filler. Most people have their own particular fillers. Try listening out for the fillers in the speech of your friends or family to see what variety of sounds, words or phrases you can identify.

The following texts and activities should help you to understand when we are most likely to use fillers and what effect they might have on the person listening to them.

Answer the questions on the following transcript. A beauty pageant contestant is responding to a question asked by a member of the audience. In this part of the competition, the contestants have an opportunity to show off their public speaking skills and to give the audience some sense of their personality, interests and values.

Key terms

Voiced pause: a pause in which the speaker makes a sound, for example 'erm'.

Filler: a word or phrase that does not appear to add much meaning but which might allow the speaker a bit of extra time to think about what they really want to say.

Context: the situation in which spoken language is used. It includes factors such as who is interacting, what their relationship is, their purpose, where they are, who is listening, what else is going on around them, and so on.

Spontaneous speech: speech that is not planned or rehearsed.

Yeah, right, erm, I think I put, ah, it in the, er, cupboard.

Audience member: recent polls have shown that a fifth of Americans can't locate the US on a world map (.) why do you think this is

Miss South Carolina: I personally believe (.) that (.) US Americans are unable to do so (.) because er some er (.) people out there in our nation don't have maps and er I believe that er our ed education like such as in South Africa and er the Iraq everywhere like such as and (.) I believe that they (.) should (.) er our education over here in the US should help the US or or should help South Africa and should help the Iraq and the Asian countries so we will be able to build up our future for our children

Activity 1

a There are lots of non-fluency features in Miss South Carolina's response on page 3.

   i How many pauses are there? Remember, they are marked by symbols such as (.) or (1).

   ii How many pauses are filled with an 'er' sound?

b Are there any other words or short phrases in her answer that you think she might be using as fillers? Pick out three examples.

c If you were a judge, what words would you use to describe Miss South Carolina's answer?

As you can see from Miss South Carolina's response, fillers can be a useful way of buying time while you try to work out what you want to say. However, sometimes these filler words, that seem meaningless on the surface, are actually used in very specific ways, as you will see in the next set of activities. The following transcript is taken from the reality TV show *The Only Way is Essex* (*TOWIE*). Lydia and Danni are having a conversation about Lydia's new boyfriend.

L: I love this stage you know like right at the beginning of a relationship and like (.) you get like all excited and like your belly goes round like a washing machine and you get all butterflies

D: I'm so happy for you

L: so we went to like this little Italian in Soho

D: aaw

L: yeah which was really nice (.) and then

D: you're blushing

L: what am I

D: yeah you're like [looks up to sky and waves head side to side] ah in the clouds

L: and then we went (.) cinema

D: aaw when you speak about him your eyes are //like (.) all// lit up

L: //do I//

D: yeah they really are you look happy have you kissed him

L: we've had like a little kiss but

D: like a peck

L: like (.) like

D: an adult kiss

L: yeah

D: yeah aaw

Activity 2

a Both Danni and Lydia make use of the filler 'like'. Who uses it more?

b What reasons might there be for the different amounts they use it in this conversation?

c Some people say that young people over-use 'like' as a filler, and that it has no meaning. However, sometimes this word is doing a little bit more than just filling the gap. Below is a list of examples where the girls use 'like' and some explanations of how the word works. Match the examples to the explanations. The first one has been done for you.

Example	Explanation of how 'like' is used
1 'you get like all excited'	A Used to introduce an impersonation of someone else.
2 'your belly goes round like a washing machine'	B Used to show something is similar, but not *exactly* the same.
3 'you're like [looks up to sky and waves head side to side] ah in the clouds'	C Used instead of 'erm', hesitating about how to respond.
4 'like a little kiss'	D Used to give some extra emphasis to the description that comes afterwards.
5 'like (.) like'	E Used to make a direct comparison between two things.

The following transcript is of two reality talent show contestants, speaking about their experiences and their relationship in an interview screened just before their first audition. Read the transcript and then attempt Activity 3 on page 6.

J: I've always had sort of problems with my size since like (.) I can remember (.) and (.) when I was in sort of primary school it was back then really that I had sort of the mick taken out of me and it it kind of damaged my confidence quite a bit (.) when when people would say something to me (1) I'd just (1) it'd just take a little piece out of me in a sense

C: I'm quite protective of Jonathan like (.) if someone (.) if I was there and someone stood there and said something to him (.) I wouldn't sit (.) I couldn't sit there with my mouth shut (.) before you make a judgement of someone I think you really need to get to know them it's not (.) as clichéd as it is it's not judging a book by its cover you've got you've got to read what's inside

J: Charlotte's been a really big help for me in terms of confidence and (.) making me a better performer and I really don't think I'd be going up on stage today if I didn't have Charlotte by my side

Activity 3

a Focus on Jonathan's speech first of all. Copy and complete the following table. Make some brief notes about the topic and the fluency of each utterance.

Jonathan's speech	What is he talking about?	How fluently does he speak? Are there any pauses or fillers or other features that disrupt the flow or meaning of his speech?
First utterance		
Second utterance		

b Look back at the notes you have made and think about the relationship between the topic and Jonathan's fluency of speech. Write a paragraph that explains how you think the two could be related. Use the following words if you need to.

- When Jonathan talks about . . .
- His speech tends to be . . .
- This may be because . . .

c Now look closely at Charlotte's utterance. You will notice that she does not speak completely fluently either. However, she still comes across as quite confident. Explain why.

Stretch yourself

Some people claim it is not 'what you say' but 'how you say it' that is important.

- What do you think of this?
- Can you think of any instances when this might be true?

Second thoughts

Have you ever started to say something and then realised, after a few words, you have not quite thought it through and decided to start all over again? You are not alone – it happens to the best of speakers. This pattern of starting, stopping and starting again is known as a **false start**. Sometimes it is a matter of simply repeating what we have already said to gain a bit more time, but sometimes we reword (or **repair**) what we have said, perhaps to make it clearer, perhaps to change the meaning ever so slightly.

Looking carefully at the little adjustments speakers make as they go along can give us clues about the speaker's intentions in the conversation. The texts and activities below will help you to understand how to interpret the way false starts and repairs work in different situations.

In the following transcript John is being interviewed for a part-time job at a restaurant. Annie is the manager of the restaurant.

Key terms

False start: where you start, stop, and then start what you are saying again. This often happens at the beginning of an utterance but it can also happen halfway through.

Repair: changing the wording of what you were originally going to say.

Annie: ok (.) right (.) you know the restaurant a bit already then so (.) what made you apply

John: well (1) I was (.) I've always done part-time waiting from when I was young from about 13 or 14 (.) but more local pubs and little places you know (.) but now we've moved into town and it's easier to get to places like this and I'd quite like to work somewhere where it's a bit more formal

Annie: formal in what sense

John: oh (.) well (.) I mean that it's form. well really smart and the food is a bit more special //and//

Annie: //mhmm//

John: the the staff always seem erm I suppose professional compared to some places like they really do a careful job and look after people

Activity 1

a There is a false start at the beginning of John's first utterance 'well (1) I was (.) I've always done part-time waiting'. Rank the possible reasons for his false start according to how important you think they are.

  i   He is nervous about the interview.

  ii   He needs a little more time to form a good answer.

  iii   He does not understand the question.

b Try to find one more example of a false start from John.

c Look closely at the example you have picked out above, paying close attention to what is said before and after his false start and the way that he repairs his phrasing. Why do you think John has a false start here?

The following transcript is of a conversation between a woman and her mother. Debbie is helping her mother Joan to fit her hearing aid.

J: it doesn't (.) the aid (.) the aid (.) //doesn't work//

D: //let's have// (1) a look (2) I think it's (2) I think it's (.) twisted (2) hold (.) hold still (1) I need to line it (.) up

J: no good (1) nothing (2) //nothing//

D: //keep still//   (*continues overleaf*)

J: it's the battery (1) is it the battery

D: no (.) no (.) that's ok (2) it needs to erm fit into your erm ear right (.) it's moulded to your erm to fit your ear

J: no (1) no (1) //nothing //

D: //it's not in// yet (1) Mum (.) Mum hold still (.) should just (1) slot in (1) there (2) how's that Mum how's that

J: what

D: can you hear me

J: yes

D: is it ok (1) comfortable

J: no (.) take it out (.) take it (.) out

D: I give up

Activity 2

a How many false starts are there in the first two utterances of this conversation?

b As well as the false starts, there are many pauses of various lengths. Think about the context of the conversation (the situation the people are in as they speak). What reasons might there be for this stop-start conversation?

c Debbie's speech becomes very fragmented (broken up) by the many pauses and false starts. Do you think it would be better if she just stayed quiet? Explain your answer.

The next transcript is of a conversation between two friends who are about to go out to a party. Anisha has been waiting while Naomi tries on a variety of outfits and she is keen to leave.

A: we need to go (.) are you gonna make a decision

N: I have

A: (1) are you really wearing that

N: what does **that** mean

A: no I didn't mean erm it **is** a nice dress

N: yeah (.) I just look //horrible// in it is //that it//

A: //no// //no no// it's nice it's nice I just thought erm (.) isn't it a bit (.) annoying for a party

N: why (.) what do you mean annoying

A: well the skirt bit is quite you know a bit big (.) puffy

N: (1) big and puffy (.) ok (.) //thanks//

A: //no I// just thought well it's (.) it is at their house isn't it

N: yeah so (.) it's a party

A: well you look quite you (.) you look quite I don't know quite dressed up (.) I just thought you might be not be very **comfy** //and//

N: //ok fine// (.) I'll get changed again then shall I

Activity 3

a   There are more non-fluency features in Anisha's speech than in Naomi's. Identify two examples and explain precisely what you think is happening in each instance. An example has been done for you.

Example of non-fluency in Anisha's speech	Description of how Anisha loses fluency here and why you think this might have happened
no I didn't mean erm it is a nice dress	*Anisha starts to defend herself and then hesitates with a voiced pause and does not finish the original sentence. It seems she decides to change strategy and says something positive instead by complimenting the dress. She might be trying to avoid having an argument.*

b   This becomes quite a tense conversation. Who do you think is more at fault and why?

c   How could this argument have been avoided? Rewrite the transcript so that Anisha still expresses her point of view in a way that does not upset Naomi.

Whose turn is it anyway?

You may have always been told it is not 'polite' to talk when someone else is talking, and it is true that in many circumstances people would find this rude. However, there are all sorts of situations when people do not take turns to speak and end up talking at the same time.

Think about the conversations that take place in your friendship group: do you always listen quietly to one another or do you sometimes interrupt and overlap in your speech? Are there certain situations when your friends are more likely to do this than at other times?

One of the ways that the flow or fluency of a conversation can be disrupted is when people do not take turns in conversation, or do not respond to each other in the way you would expect. This might involve overlapping someone else's speech, interrupting them, ignoring them or changing the subject.

The texts and activities that follow will help you to understand how and why conversations can become uneven or out of sequence. You will also see that some types of overlapping are more disruptive than others.

The following transcript involves three brothers, Kevin, Nick and Joe, who are in a band together. They are telling the story of an event that took place at a performance the night before. The brothers are talking via webcam to an online audience of their fans.

K: oh my gosh (.) **coolest** story **ever** about the show last night (1) //you were there//

N: //oh yeah oh yeah//

K: ok I get to tell it //I get to tell it I//

J: //oh cool we should we should//

N: //we're gonna put it up on YouTube// today

K: are we really

N: I think we are

J: we should just bring the video in here and show everybody

K: //ah well//

N: //we won't// worry about that

K: check it out this is the way it's gonna happen (1) so (.) it was //unbelievable//

N: //this is what// happened

K: we were all in the centre ring //we're spinning around//

J: //waah waah awesome//

K: and all of a sudden Nick finishes burning up he's like **bam** I'm done with the song and all of a sudden this dude in the audience gets this pair of sunglasses from //these two girls//

N: //it wasn't out// of anger or //anything//

K: //oh no//

N: he wasn't being mean or anything

K: he was //he was just trying to (.) because the girls said//

J: //he was trying to give Nick a nice pair of yellow// sunglasses (.)

K: so what he did //was//

J: //lime green//

K: […] took these sunglasses and he chucked them as hard as he could (.) and literally (.) they come flying they were like //[rotates hands and makes sound effect]//

J: //amazing//

K: right into Nick's hand like right at Nick's face and he just bam grabs it (.) and then like pulls it and like breaks the glasses and throws them on the ground

N: well I grabbed them so tight in my hands they cracked and then I threw them on the ground

K: it was literally the most like (.) James Bond moment I think you've ever //had//

N: //it was// it was pretty crazy

Activity 1

a

i Work in a group of three. Try to read the transcript aloud. There are not many pauses, so it is quite a fast-paced conversation. You need to try to speak at the same time when there is an overlap. You may need to try it a few times to get it right.

ii Now that you have read the transcript, which word do you think would best describe the **tone** of the interaction? Tick the word you think is most appropriate.

Tone	Tick
Tense	
Miserable	
Friendly	
Irritable	
Lively	

b Look again at the transcript and imagine what it would sound like to listen to. If you had been one of the fans watching and listening online, what problems might you have?

c The brothers overlap each other a lot but this is not always a bad thing. Sometimes they overlap to clarify and to support what the other person is saying. Try to find some examples in the transcript of these types of overlap:

● clarifying – rephrasing or adding to what is being said to make the story clearer

● supporting – saying the same thing, maybe in a slightly different way to back up and agree with what is being said.

Key term

Tone: refers to the emotions behind a speaker's utterance. Tone is created by the sound of your voice, by the pitch, pace and speed that you talk at, and even by the words you choose.

As you have seen, in some circumstances (particularly when the speakers have a close relationship), overlapping can be an acceptable part of conversation. However, it is less acceptable in more formal situations. The transcript on page 12 is of an interaction which took place at a local committee meeting.

Ms Martin wants to discuss the responsibilities of certain members of the committee. She has raised this issue at a previous meeting, it has been discussed and the committee have already voted once before that they will keep things as they are.

You will notice there are several examples of overlapping in this conversation. It could be said that these are more like interruptions, as participants are butting in before the other person has finished speaking. Look closely at the moments of overlap, marked by the //.

Mr Bhatt:	next item on the agenda (.) resolution determining committee roles and responsibilities
Ms Martin:	(2) ok well I'll make that motion
Mr Bhatt:	motion made by Ms Martin (2) we're waiting for a second (6) still waiting for a second
Mr Wilson:	you ought to know you're not going to get one
Ms Martin:	it needs discussion //so that//
Ms Hewitt:	//no one// wants to discuss this now
Mr Bhatt:	I think (.) //it would be better//
Mr Wilson:	//you've already// made your speech (.) and frankly (.) we don't need to hear it again (.) you're not going to get a second on this
Ms Martin:	//but this//
Ms Hewitt:	//so the// motion **fails**
Mr Bhatt:	hold on (.) we must follow procedure here
Ms Hewitt:	sorry but but the motion fails for lack of a second
Mr Bhatt:	hmm
Ms Hewitt:	it fails for a //lack of//
Mr Bhatt:	//I **understand**// Ms Hewitt
Ms Hewitt:	so how long are you going to wait (.) I'm just asking the question how long are you gonna wait
Mr Bhatt:	well (2) I'm still waiting for a second (5) //still waiting for a second//
Mr Wilson:	//this is ridiculous//
Ms Hewitt:	Chairman is there any time limit on (.) how long you have to wait before a motion fails for lack of a second (.) or are we going to sit here till midnight
Mr Bhatt:	there's no time limit the the committee has the right to make a motion as it does in all other //instances//
Ms Hewitt:	//ok fine// (.) is there any procedure er that we can do to end this

Mr Bhatt: well of course if the committee determines that the time needed for making a motion is over someone can make a motion to determine that there has been no second and move on to the next //item//

Ms Hewitt: //ok// I'll make that motion that there has been no second ample time has been given and er it fails for lack of a second

Ms Olson: I'll second

Ms Hewitt: thank you (1) so can we vote please and move on

Activity 2

a Copy and complete the table, counting up how many times each person speaks, how many times they interrupt others and how many times they are interrupted.

	Number of times this person speaks	Number of times this person starts speaking when someone else is talkling	Number of times this person gets talked over by someone else before they have finished
Mr Bhatt			
Ms Martin			
Mr Wilson			
Ms Hewitt			
Ms Olson			

b Based on the information in your table and your interpretation of the conversation, who do you think are the two most powerful individuals at this meeting? Explain in detail why you have chosen these two.

c What do you think is the best way to deal with someone who interrupts all the time? Explain how you would deal with this in:

i an informal situation (e.g. when chatting with your friends)

ii a formal situation (e.g. in a school council meeting).

If you are working with others, compare your suggestions and decide which of your strategies you think would work best.

The following transcript involves an interaction between a mother (M), father (F), their 12-year-old daughter Katie (K) and their baby son Tom. The conversation takes place in the morning as the family have breakfast and prepare for the day ahead.

M: here (4) there (.) here we are (.) slowly (2)

F: Tom (2) //Thomas//

M: //come on// Tom (.) there's a good careful

F: what a mess

M: there we go (.) is it good Tom (.) is (.) does it taste nice Tom (.) that's right all in Tom's tummy (2)

F: what's school what have you got at school today (1) Katie

M: listen to him (.) yummy yummy Tom's tummy

F: are you getting the eight ten (.) sorry school Katie

K: well there's science (4)

F: what are you doing in (.) science

K: leaves and things (2)

F: you getting the eight ten

M: uh huh

F: what have you learnt //about leaves//

M: //there we go//

K: photosynthesis

M: just like that

F: what's photosynthesis then

M: um what's photosynthesis Katie

K: the sun and the leaves (.) something

F: Tom

M: just the one more (.) what does the sun do (.) to leaves

K: erm (.) makes them grow (.) and makes them green (.) chlorophyll or something

M: well let's get you all done

F: right

M: well trees are very important (.) aren't they Tom

Activity 3

a As you read through this conversation you may find it difficult to make sense of it at times because the utterances do not follow each other in a logical sequence. Part of the reason for this is that there is more than one interaction taking place but they have become mixed together. Complete the grid below to help sort out the different threads of conversation.

Who ...	Talking to ...	About ...
Mother	Tom	The breakfast she is feeding him

b Look closely at the moments Katie speaks. Describe what usually happens straight after she speaks.

c Imagine you were in Katie's position. How might you feel during this conversation? Give reasons for your answer.

Speaking and listening

The study of spoken language is a relatively new part of GCSE courses and it should give you some very beneficial knowledge and skills.

Working with a partner, discuss how you could use your understanding of spoken interaction in other areas of your English study. Could there be any other real-life or practical ways that your knowledge of spoken language might come in useful?

Check your learning

In this unit you have learned about some of the non-fluency features commonly found in spoken language. Look at this extract of conversation between a teacher and her four-year-old pupil. Use the terms you have learned to describe some of the non-fluency features in this interaction. Each time you describe a feature, try to explain why it is important and why the speaker may have lost fluency at that particular point.

T: Daniel (.) can you come to me please (3) I'm really sad to see this (2) really really sad to see this ruler's broken

D: yeah well it **was** an accident I was erm only playing

T: but what on (.) what //what were you doing//

D: //I didn't know//

T: but what //were you// **doing**

D: //oh (.) well//

T: because you must have had to do something very **hard** to make this break

D: I (1) I hit it on that wall

Interaction and the structure of talk: Following the rules

H ave you ever wondered why we say some things even if we do not really need to say them? For example, if you bump into someone that you do not know very well, and they say hello, you often find yourself asking 'How are you?' Do you care how they are? Probably not, but you do it just the same. This is just one example of how interaction works; we follow a set of unwritten rules that help conversations to work. This unit aims to show you how to describe some of the patterns and structures in spoken language, as well as to explore how the context of the conversation can affect these patterns.

Here is a radio interview where Tulisa speaks about her new album *Young*.

This is a good example of an opening sequence. The conversation is divided into pairs, where each person's question or comment definitely requires a response. It would be very disheartening to be met with silence after saying 'hello'. When Clara asks Tulisa 'Are you good?', she is assuming that Tulisa probably is well but the question is a way of warming up before the actual interview. This sort of talk is called phatic talk and describes the unnecessary small talk which makes up much of our conversations.

The laughter can be called **back-channelling**, it allows Tulisa to know that her comments are appreciated and that she can carry on talking.

Latching on (=) here shows that the participants are involved in a cooperative conversation where they support each other's attempt at conversation.

C: ok so the female boss is in the Kiss building, it's Tulisa

T: hello

C: are you good

T: I'm good how are you?

C: I'm fine thank you (.) so at this moment how are you feeling right now

T: a bit tired

C: laughs

T: I'm always a bit tired at the minute but no I'm all right

C: but tiredness is good it means you're still working (.) still doing it=

T: =exactly (.) I'm getting a few days off so I'm looking forward to that now

C: what you gonna do on your days off

T: literally just go to sleep and chill out with mates and just //relax//

C: //and// just sleep

Clara interrupts Tulisa, but you can tell by the way that she repeats 'sleep' that she is encouraging Tulisa's story.

Key term

Back-channelling: the supportive words or sounds that are used to indicate that we are listening and interested in a conversation.

Latching on (=): describes conversations where there is no gap between the participant's utterances. A bracket with a dot in the middle (.) is a short pause.

T: sleep a lot (.) sleep a lot and eat food and //watch DVDs//

C: //you're a girl// after my own heart like the sound of that now last time I interviewed you it was about a year ago (.) X Factor was just about to air (.) you were hinting about this solo career that you have started now and now here you are so has the past year kind of surpassed your expectations

T: definitely what I can't me (.) I can't complain what a year it's just been amazing obviously with everything from the X Factor um to now releasing my solo stuff it's just a whirlwind like I dunno pinch me someone pinch me I dunno //what's going on//

C: //I can't quite reach over//

T: there you go=

C: =there you go it's real=

C: on that note Tulisa thank you very much for hanging with us

T: thank you for having me

C: May 7th all about it (.) Young (.) go get it

T: wicked

Clara is friendly but her role as the interviewer means that she has to guide the conversation to its main **transactional** purpose, which is to find out about Tulisa's new album. She changes topic with the word 'Now'.

These two words, 'surpassed' and 'amazing', are used to maintain interest for the listeners, the use of **hyperbole** shows the listeners that Tulisa is very successful and that they are very lucky to hear an interview with such a busy and high-profile star.

Key terms

Transactional: when language has a message as its main focus.

Hyperbole: an exaggerated statement.

Cue: language that acts as a prompt.

Metaphorical language also creates interest in her story.

The closing sequence also follows a set pattern; both participants understand how to end the conversation and what the signals mean.

Opening and closing cues

The first aspect of interaction that we are going to look at is how people start and finish conversations.

Once a conversation has started, we follow **cues** that tell us whether we should carry on speaking. There are certainly some instances in which it would be unusual to continue talking and some where it is expected. For example, if you are in a classroom and your teacher says, 'Right, well today I'm going to start off by explaining the grade boundaries for your exam', it would be unusual to reply by saying something like, 'Oh, thanks Sir, I've been looking forward to that.' On the other hand, if your teacher came into the classroom and said directly to you, 'Have you remembered to bring the Poetry Anthology today?' it would seem very rude if you just ignored him.

As well as knowing how to reply to starting cues, we usually understand when to continue talking in a conversation and when it is appropriate to stop. Look at this example.

B: can I help

A: two cokes and a blueberry muffin please

B: anything else

A: no thanks

B: £5.80 then

A: there you go

B: thanks and 20 pence change

A: thanks bye

B: have a good day

Although neither of the people in the conversation know each other, they both understand that they are expected to answer in a certain way. By asking if A wants help, B is opening the conversation and A knows exactly what to say next; her order.

Everything that B says is guided by her job and her questions are all practical. However, once the money has changed hands, there is no actual need for either of them to say anything. The line 'there you go' is friendly more than necessary and leads to a series of polite turns afterwards. By saying goodbye, both parties realise that the conversation does not have to go on any further.

Activity 1

a Can you think of words that require a response from you in conversation? Copy the table and fill in the missing replies. Add some more of your own.

Utterance	Expected reply
Looking good!	*Thanks*
How are you?	
Hello	
See you later	

b If you are working with other people, compare their answers with yours. Are they similar?

c i Look at the following snippets of conversation (Text A and Text B) and identify which one is expected to continue and which one is finished. Try to describe how you know.

Activity 1 cont.

Text A

A: that's two pounds and seventy pence change

B: thanks

A: thank you bye

Text B

A: have you got change for a fiver

B: well(.) I'll have to //open// the till so …

A: //he// won't let me on the bus with a note

ii Can you think of ways in which A in Text B could end the conversation? Write out the conversation with your own ending.

Often when we start conversations, we say things that do not actually carry much meaning. These words and phrases are called **phatic communication** and are really important in a conversation in terms of keeping it going.

Think about this example. You have travelled for a couple of hours to see a relation who you do not meet very often. Although you would probably have lots of interesting things to talk about, you are unlikely to jump straight into these topics. Instead you are more likely to talk about your journey (Was it a good journey? Did you get held up?), maybe your relation's appearance (I like your hair, have you had it cut?) or even the weather (Isn't it lovely out? We're really lucky.). None of these conversations are particularly important but they allow you to get used to each other again.

Look at the following conversation and then attempt Activity 2 on page 20. Sam and Mark from *The Only Way is Essex* have had a relationship previously and so they know each other well. Even so, there are lots of examples of phatic communication.

> **Key term**
>
> **Phatic communication:** a type of warming up; you are getting yourself ready for the demands of the person that you are talking to and the context of the talk.

S: hello

M: how you doin'

S: good thanks you (3) mm make-up looks good

M: how you getting on

S: not bad

M: you look nice

S: thanks

M: good outfit

a Can you identify which words and phrases could be classed as phatic communication?

b Sometimes the type of phatic communication can help us to work out how people in the conversation feel about each other. Can you match the statement with a part of the transcript which backs it up?

  i   Mark finds Sam attractive.

  ii Sam has something on her mind.

  iii The couple are alone.

c Think of a similar scenario. A boyfriend and girlfriend have just met and so a conversation begins. Script two different openings for these conversations: one in which the boyfriend is planning to tell his girlfriend some disappointing news, the other in which he is going to tell her some good news.

Focus on the beginning, without any of the actual 'news' being discussed, and compare how your use of phatic communication varies according to the context.

Telephone conversations seem particularly ritualised at times. Because you cannot see the facial expressions of the person that you are talking to, you have to rely on the spoken word alone to understand if someone is tired, bored, excited or upset. Also, because we do not know what the other person is doing, or where they are, we have to use words very clearly to explain how we want the conversation to proceed.

Think about your own conversations on the phone. Do they usually start with the same sort of words? The same is the case with endings. You cannot see someone looking at their watch to suggest that they need to finish the conversation, instead you rely on certain ending cues which allow each person to understand that it is time to stop talking.

As you can see in the following transcript, both people want to finish the conversation but they tend to give signals as to this rather than say it directly ('it's been great catching up', rather than 'I want to go now').

A: it's been great catching up

B: yes, we'll definitely have to meet up soon

A: yes, not leave it so long (.) so I //better//

B: //yes// it's really late (.) bye then (.) love to everyone

A: bye (.) yes and love to yours

B: bye

Some ending cues are more businesslike but they still avoid being abrupt. For example:

A: I think that I've got all that I need now so thanks for your help

B: no problem. Is there anything else that I can help you with

A: no (.) that's fine

B: goodbye then and thank you for calling

A: thanks (.) bye

This example is typical of many conversations that you may have on the phone if you call an organisation or business. These conversations follow strict patterns, partly because employees are taught to speak on the phone in a particular way. Funnily enough, we soon adapt to these patterns ourselves.

The conversation below is between two lovers who are obviously finding it hard to be the first person to put the phone down. Read the ending and then work through the activities that follow.

M: night darling (.) sounds like you're dragging an enormous piece of string behind you with hundreds of tin pots and cans attached to it (.) I think it will be your telephone (.) night night before the battery goes (blows kiss) night

W: love you

M: don't want to say goodbye

W: neither do I (.) but we must get some sleep (.) bye

M: bye darling

W: love you (.) hopefully talk to you in the morning

M: please

W: love you forever

M: g'bye (.) bye my darling

W: bye (.) press the button

M: going to press the button

W: (yawns) love you (.) night

M: adore you (.) night

W: (blows a kiss)

M: night

W: g'night my darling

Activity 3

a What do you think the purpose of this conversation is?

b A lot of this conversation is made up of pairs. Copy and complete the table below to show how many pairs are made up of the same words.

Woman	Man
Bye	Bye darling

c Rewrite the conversation so that W wants to finish the conversation but M does not. Remember to think about the way that people use cues to signal endings.

Where am I? Transactional, interactional and context

Some conversations have a very specific purpose and this means that they will be structured in a specific way. For example, you might ask your teacher for a book, you might ask a friend for a pen. These conversations are called transactional because there is a specific outcome. However, lots of conversations do not have a specific outcome; we just talk because it is a social activity. These conversations are called **interactional**.

Key terms

Interactional: when the social relationships are more important than the message.

The table below gives you an idea of which sorts of conversations are interactional and which sorts are transactional. However, it is worth being aware that many conversations have elements of both in them. They might begin as being transactional but end up as being interactional.

Transactional	Interactional
Buying a meal from a fast food restaurant	Talking to your friend who works in the restaurant about how busy he has been today
Ringing a friend to ask them what you have to do for your maths homework	Talking to your friend about the seating plan that you hate in maths
Organising a trip to the cinema with your friends	Discussing the film afterwards

Read the openings of the following conversations. Then answer the questions which ask you to consider the purpose of a conversation and its topic. Are the two always the same?

Text 1
In a greengrocer's

A: isn't it bitter (.) really cold

B: really cold (.) yeah so (.) haven't seen a spring like it for years

A: no (.) years

Text 2
At home

A: are you watching this (1)

B: shut the door

A: oh you're nice

B: shut it

A: I want to watch *Friends*

Text 3
In the canteen

A: do you know where the French workroom is (.)

B: no (.) don't do French um it's on the third floor I think

A: oh (.) I'll try up there then

Activity 1

a   What is the topic of each conversation?

b   Are the conversations interactional or transactional?

c   What would you say is the actual purpose of each conversation?

The following transcript is a good example of how a transactional conversation turns into an interaction conversation. It takes place in Anna's bedroom. Also in the room are Anna's 10-year-old sister, Sarah, and Sarah's friend Mary. By looking at how the girls talk to each other as well as what they are talking about, you can comment on how spoken language allows us to form relationships.

A: anyway (.) as my website was great (.) I had like seven different pages Leah had only five

L: //I wasn't here for one of them//

A: //so// (.) you could have done two pages=

L: =I did, I did more than that (.) I had like seven or eight (.) //more than you//

A: //Ooh you// embarrassed me in front of the tape

S: our one's called //stars site//

A: //anyway// mine had loads of information Leah's just was all just like Olly Murs' middle //name//

L: //I had//

S: //ooh// what's Olly Murs' middle name (.) I don't //know//

L: //and other// stuff

A: oh yeah I have like lots of events and stuff (.) you can have your birthday party there right next to the llamas um you can have your wedding and it says something like this er do I hear wedding bells ringing=

L: =you decide=

A: =the lions roaring=

L: =(laughing) you decide

Activity 2

a   What do you think is the topic of the conversation?

b   What can you tell about the girls' relationships? What evidence have you got for this point of view?

c   Is the topic any different to the purpose?

The following is the opening of a radio phone-in show about sport. Here we are going to focus on exploring how the presenters adapt their opening in order to interest their listeners.

Radio presenters have to use language that will engage their listeners

JC: hello good evening and welcome to the Sports Bar here on talkSPORT with me Jason Cundy and my wingman for the next 3 hours Mr Sam Delaney coming between now and 1 am we'll be discussing Andy Carroll (.) I know we broke the news last night but it looks like a likely move away from Anfield (.) Liverpool fans do you want to see him go and West Ham Chairman David Sullivan has said that he wants to take him on (.) would you have him at your club call 08717 22 33 44

SD: we will also be joined by new Reading signing Nicky Shorey and taking your calls on tonight's match between England and Australia (.) all that plus tomorrow's back pages.

Activity 3

a The DJs try to make the audience feel welcome. Can you match the techniques used by the DJs with these examples from the text?

Welcome to the Sports Bar	Direct address
Would you have him at your club?	Phatic communication
Taking your calls	**Interrogative** sentences

b Jason and Sam try to set up an imaginary meeting place for listeners to discuss their sporting ideas. What **metaphors** can you find to see how this world is made appealing?

c The use of pronouns is important in creating a relationship with the listeners. Copy and complete the following grid to show how pronouns are used in the transcript.

Pronoun and term	Effect
'me' Jason Cundy, first-person pronoun	Making it clear to the audience who is talking

Key terms

Interrogative: a sentence that acts as a question.

Metaphor: a word or expression that suggests a comparison with something else but which is not meant literally.

If a presenter uses a pronoun such as 'us' or 'our' it involves the listener and encourages them to think that they have a shared interest with the presenter and the other listeners. Similarly, if a pronoun such as 'you' is used, the listeners are invited to be involved with the programme. This is especially the case with talk radio, where the programmes rely on listeners being moved to call the show and air their views.

Maintaining interest

So, we now know that the ways in which we begin and end conversations follow certain rules and we know that the context of the conversation, where it is set or its purpose, can also affect the structure of the conversation. Now we are going to explore how conversations are maintained after the initial opening. Remember to still think about the purpose of conversations when you first read them, as well as the opening and closing cues.

When we have conversations both participants work at keeping the talk going so that it builds into a conversation rather than disconnected questions and answers. Words and phrases that seem meaningless like 'yeah' and 'really' or even just laughter are useful in telling our audience that we are still listening and that we want them to carry on talking. This is called back-channelling. Of course, they can also show that we are not very interested. I am sure that you can think of an example where 'really' can be used sarcastically.

A: how's your mum and dad

B: fine

A: is your mum still working (.) at the post office

B: no

A: oh (.) when did she leave

B: dunno

Activity 1

a Imagine how you would feel if you were participant A. Write three or four **adjectives** to describe your feelings about B.

b So, we know that what we do not say sometimes has a bigger impact on our audience than the actual words that we use. Can you adapt the conversation from above to make it seem more fluent?

c Look back at your changes. Can you see any patterns in the types of words or structures that you used to keep the talk fluent?

> **Key term**
>
> **Adjective:** a word used to describe a noun.

Most people in a conversation try hard to keep it going. We also find it very hard to talk if we do not experience feedback. Read the following transcript and answer the questions that follow.

C: I had a tat (.) of his name

H: (laughs)

C: and two weeks later we split up

H: two weeks

C: yeah had it and almost broke up straight away

H: did you (.) god two weeks

C: yeah an (.) and then it was like (.) I can't believe it

H: really

Activity 2

a Identify examples of back-channelling in the conversation.

b Choose one of your examples of back-channelling. Can you explain the impact that back-channelling has on C's telling of the story?

c Try to think of other examples of words that could be called back-channelling. Do they always have the same effect as in the tattoo story? You can use a chart like the one below to record your findings.

Context	Back-channel word or phrase	Effect on conversation
Phone call to grandparent	Oh goodness	Politely shows that grandchild is listening

The following transcript is an interview. Back-channelling is not just important in social and interactional conversations. In the interview below it is used in order to encourage a nervous interviewee to speak at length.

Director: the company's been going for about **24 years** (.) did you look us up on the website

Interviewee: I did **yeah yeah** (.) yes I did actually {clears throat} it's a global company so (.) erm when your assistant rang me I said I was interested in gettin' into a global company again (.) cause it's quite big // and//

The director initiates the conversation by using a direct question. Although this might put the interviewee under pressure, it also allows them to prove how much research they have done.

Director: //yeah//

Interviewee: and you do get obviously //take a// (.) great amount of **calls** and everything

The use of back-channelling 'yeah' which overlaps the interviewee's answer, show that she is doing well and answering the question in the right way.

Director: //yep yep//

Interviewee: and it's //it's a busy **role** and//

Director: //yeah absolutely very//

Interviewee: and I you know I used to run two switchboards in the one (.) for Barclays at Gadbrook **Park** and erm (.) the Peterborough one so one was erm (.) you know for wills and that and the other is (.) //an investment so//

Director: //OK mm hmm//

Interviewee: I took anything up to (.) 300 //calls a day//

Director: //right OK//

Interviewee: as well as multi tasking=

Director: =yeah, yeah, oh absolutely

Activity 3

a What do you think the director wants to achieve with this conversation?

b List examples of back-channelling.

c Choose two examples of back-channelling and explain, in full sentences, their impact in the conversation. You can use the example to help model your answer.

When we listen to somebody's story, as well as using back-channelling to show that we are actively listening, the person telling the story uses language in an attempt to keep the story interesting. In the chat show interview on page 28 both participants are trying to keep their live audience interested. You can tell from the use of latching on (=) that both participants are keen to keep the conversation cooperative.

Jake (J): that looks like a pretty nasty injury you have there (.) it's your leg I'm guessing (.) right

Daniel (D): yes

J: so how did you injure yourself

D: um playing for my local team (.) Dagenham Old Boys (.) I went to knock it round the guy and just felt this searing pain and collapsed and the back of my leg was like (.) on fire (.) really really burning and I realised I'd done my er hammy y'know

J: actually completely tore your hamstring muscle (.) torn (.) goodness (.) what a nightmare and er at what point did you know it was serious=

D: straight away (.) straight away er soon as I tried to get back up and play on (.) I felt the rip and er looked down and er I could feel the burning in my thigh spreading all down my leg

J: wow

D: I know (.) yeah (.) proper nasty

J: I was gonna ask you about that that's what people always say (.) and it truly was the experience=

D: yeah (.) yeah

J   and perhaps one of the most painful injuries a footballer can endure

Stretch yourself

a   Make a list of words or phrases that the host, Jake, uses to show his interest in the conversation.

b   Make a list of the words that are repeated in the transcript. What effect do they have in maintaining the audience's attention?

c   As well as repetition, what do the participants say to make the story as dramatic as possible?

But ... don't interrupt!

Sometimes the structure of a conversation, rather than the actual topic, can show you the feelings of the participants. If you think about your conversations, you know that sometimes you interrupt to show enthusiasm and agreement and sometimes to show frustration or disagreement. We also use our knowledge of context when we choose to interrupt; there are some circumstances when it would be too rude to do it. For example, it probably would not be considered rude if you interrupted your brother or sister in the morning to ask them if they have seen your PE kit:

Sister:	so is it OK if I go straight from school tonight
Mum:	sure
Sister:	cos there's this
Brother:	//has anyone seen my trainers//
Sister:	//try the car (.) there's this really nice dress I want to try on

However, in a different context, to interrupt would be rude:

Mum:	we haven't had any hot water for 24 hours now so it's urgent
Plumber:	problem is the part you see we don't//
Brother:	//where are my trainers

By looking at how the conversation is built with questions, repetition and new topics, we can work out how people feel about each other, the situation and the topic being discussed. Many playwrights draw on their knowledge of spontaneous speech in order to create believable characters and exciting conversations. Here we use *Oleanna* to look at how everyday language can be used for dramatic effect.

The following transcript is an excerpt from a play. John is a university lecturer and Carol is his student. She has visited his office because she feels that she needs help in understanding the language used on the course.

The ways in which topics are changed are also an interesting way of looking at the structure of conversation. As well as interrupting, people can show their disagreement by changing the topic.

Oleanna
David Mamet

John: There are problems, as there usually are, about the final agreements for the new house.

Carol: You're buying a new house.

John: That's right.

Carol: Because of your promotion.

John: Well, I suppose that's right.

Carol: Why did you stay here with me?   (*Continues overleaf*)

John: Stay here.

Carol: Yes. When you should have gone.

John: Because I like you.

Carol: You like me.

John: Yes.

Carol: Why?

John: Why? Well? Perhaps we're similar (pause) Yes (pause)

Carol: You said 'everyone has problems.'

Activity 1

a Read this section from *Oleanna* and look at how the topic is changed and the words used to do this. Highlight when the topic changes.

b Who changes the topic most of the time?

c Look at the list of adjectives below. Which ones do you think describe Carol's behaviour in this short extract? Can you explain why?

- Blunt
- Unfriendly
- Nervous
- Serious
- Cautious

Activity 2

a Make a list of all instances of repetition in the transcript.

b Why do you think David Mamet has written the play like this? Why does John seem to mirror what Carol is saying? Choose from the reasons below and explain your choice.

Why does John mirror what Carol is saying?	Do you agree? Explain why, or why not
Because he is confused and he was not expecting this type of conversation with Carol.	
Because he cannot think of anything else to say.	
Because he is trying to diffuse the situation. Repeating Carol's lines buys him time.	

c It was suggested above that the structure of conversation can reveal much about the characters' feelings. Is this true in *Oleanna*? By looking at the following extract, can you explain how you think Carol feels about John and how John feels about Carol?

John: No one thinks you're stupid.

Carol: No? What am I . . .?

John: I . . .

Carol: . . . what am I, then?

Activity 2 cont.

John: I think you're angry. Many people are. I have a telephone call that I have to make. And an appointment, which is rather pressing; though I sympathise with your concerns, and though I wish I had the time, this was not a previously scheduled meeting and I . . .

Carol: . . . you think I'm nothing. . .

John: . . . have an appointment with a realtor, and with my wife and. . .

Carol: You think that I'm stupid.

John: No. I certainly don't.

Carol: You said it.

John: No I did not.

Carol: You did.

John: When?

Carol: . . . you . . .

John: No. I never did, or never would say that to a student, and . . .

Carol: You said, 'What can that mean?' (pause) 'What can that mean?'. . .

Check your learning

For this role play, you need to work with a partner. Imagine that one of you is a teacher and the other is a student. The student has come to see the teacher to get help with their homework. However, the student has an agenda; they do not like the way that the teacher has explained the subject. The teacher is surprised and at first tries to help, then tries to end the conversation without appearing too rude.

To stretch yourselves, try to use some speech styles similar to those of David Mamet. These could be:

- repetition of key words
- unusual changes of topic for the student
- the teacher copying and repeating some of the student's words and phrases
- the teacher trying to make excuses to finish the conversation
- the student not behaving as is expected.

1 Circle examples of interruptions and overlapping.

2 Can you explain whether these interruptions or overlaps are angry or friendly?

3 Who do you think is more dominant in the conversation? Does the person who interrupts the most necessarily have the most power?

Lexis: The words we use

Lexis: a technical term for words or vocabulary.

Informal: describes language that is casual, friendly or unofficial.

Subject-specific: any words that are closely connected to a specialist subject.

Jargon: special words or phrases including subject-specific words that are used by a particular profession or group.

In this unit you will look at the words people choose when they are interacting with different people in different situations. The words we select can reveal all sorts of things about our background, our attitude, our interests, our knowledge and our relationship with the person or people we are talking to.

An annotated example

In the following transcript, a hairstylist is consulting a new client about how she would like her hair cut. The overall purpose of this conversation is to agree on a style, but the stylist also wants to make the new client feel comfortable about the experience. Their word choices link to the situation and purpose of the conversation.

*The stylist opens the conversation in an **informal** way using 'we' to make the client feel as though they are working together.*

*Both the stylist and the client use **subject-specific** words from the field of hairdressing.*

*Here the stylist uses several technical terms to describe the different types of 'bob' haircuts he can create. He is showing off his knowledge and giving the client confidence in his ability by using this type of **jargon**.*

The stylist wants the client to look forward to the cut she will have so he uses lots of positive adjectives ('nice', 'simple', 'perfect') so she understands the process and can imagine the end haircut.

H: right then what we doing with this haircut

C: right well basically most of the hair like you know coming off it's getting a bit

H: so you're taking (.) right then so how much length are we talking about

C: erm probably to start off with because you can kind of see where I've dyed and highlighted it before kind of up to there

H: so we're talking about a sort of bobby-type length

C: erm yeah kind of a bob but not so much of a bob //in itself//

H: //no//

C: so it's got more //build in it//

H: //no I know but there// are all sorts of variation of bob there's a one-length bob there's a graduated bob there's a layered bob there's a textured bob yeah (1) so what I think we should do then

C: mhmm

H: is put in a nice one length

C: yeah

H: put in a simple few layers

C: mhmm

H: blow-dry it get it perfect and straight

C: mhmm

H: and then texture it (.) and what you'll end up with (.) is a sort of nice dicey

*Words like 'dicey' and 'choppy' have **connotations** of movement which is the look he is trying to achieve.*

C: yeah

H: choppy textured little number

*The stylist maintains his informal tone throughout. **Colloquial** expressions like 'little number' show he is at ease and this helps to make the client feel more comfortable too.*

C: mhmm

H: it's not gonna be one length and boring

C: fabulous yeah

The client becomes more positive in response to the description of her new hairstyle.

H: but at the same time it's not gonna be layered to death

The stylist uses an informal metaphor to exaggerate what could happen if he cut too many layers into the client's hair.

Review and reflect

In this transcript, it seems as though the hair stylist manages to reassure the client through their word choices.

Write a short script (10–15 lines) in which a patient goes to see their doctor about their sore throat. Remember, the doctor will want to reassure their patient.

When you have finished, look back over your script and annotate your own work, labelling any specific types of words that you think you have used to suit the context.

Getting technical

Think about the way people talk in the kinds of medical dramas you see on TV. As the paramedic rushes the patient through A&E, she introduces him to the doctor: 'This is Terry Davis, mid-forties, found collapsed, extensive cardiac history, two previous MIs, short of breath, sats 75 per cent, given him some GTN, query LVF.'

In a similar way, a mechanic might be heard to go into detail when explaining to the customer the problems with his car: 'We've got to the bottom of the EML. You had sludge in your filter head and the head gasket's gone.'

This kind of subject-specific or specialist language is sometimes called jargon. But why do people get technical in this way?

There is no single answer to this. People use specialist language for all sorts of reasons. Sometimes it can help two people who have a lot of knowledge on a subject to talk more efficiently. Sometimes it can help to be more precise. Sometimes it can be used to confuse and intimidate people. Sometimes people use it to show off.

Key terms

Connotations: the ideas or feelings associated with a particular word.

Colloquial: describes language that is chatty and informal but which everyone can understand.

Professions such as architect require in-depth knowledge of subject-specific language

Speaking and listening

Work with a partner. Think about your own hobbies and interests. Discuss whether there any words or phrases connected to your special areas of interest that you understand and can use confidently but that other people might not be able to?

The following transcript is of the introduction to a lecture on science given by a physics professor to some GCSE science students.

Scientists like Professor Brian Cox use technical terminology in their spoken langauge

thank you **all** for (.) coming today [...] the aim of these lectures is to [...] just cover a **few** of the things that you're gonna be (.) learning about and working on in your GCSE (.) Science just a few of the topics that **we** thought were interesting and you would perhaps want a little bit more **depth** and a little bit more (.) **detail** about erm topics like the formation of the moon er (.) topics like the the earth's magnetic field and what it does for us and how it creates the the northern lights and also (.) er going all the way back to the start of the universe the big bang (.) so what is the evidence for the big bang what (.) **was** it when did it happen (.) but most crucially (.) how do we know

Later in the lecture the professor says:

I know that (.) some of you will have (.) learnt about **isotopes** (.) of different **elements** which (.) if you get an element like carbon (.) for example which has **six** protons (.) and **six** neutrons in it (.) that's called carbon-12 because it's got 12 protons and neutrons all put together (.) you can also have a thing called carbon-14 (.) which has **six** protons and **eight** neutrons (.) that's called a different **isotope** same for oxygen and in **fact** (.) it turns out that the **ratio** of these different forms of oxygen in rocks is **very** (.) sensitive it can be very sensitively measured and at different places in the solar system er when planets formed closer to the sun or further away from the sun you find different ratios of these things

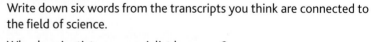

Activity 1

a   Write down six words from the transcripts you think are connected to the field of science.

b   Why do scientists use specialist language?
   i   They are trained to talk like this.
   ii   They need specialist words to talk about their subject precisely.
   iii   They like to make other people feel stupid.

c   The professor uses less specialist language at the beginning of the lecture than he does later on. Why might this be a good idea?

The following extract is from a play called *Kes*. In the extract Billy, a school pupil, has been asked by his teacher, Mr Farthing, to explain his new hobby to the class. He has been training a kestrel falcon which he found in the woods.

Billy goes out to the front of the class hesitatingly.

MF: Right, how did you set about training it?

B: I started training Kes when I'd had him about a fortnight. He was as fat as a pig though at first. You can't do much with them until you've got their weight down. Gradually you cut their food down, until you go in one time and they're keen. I could tell with Kes because he jumped straight on my glove as I held it towards him. So while he was feeding I got hold of his jesses.

MF: His what?

B: Jesses. He wears them on his legs all the time so you can get hold of them as he sits on your glove.

MF: And how do you spell that?

B: J-E-S-S-E-S.

MF: Right, tell us more.

B: Then when he's on your glove you get the swivel – like a swivel on a dog lead, then you thread your leash – that's a leather thong – through your swivel, do you see?

MF: Yes, I see. Carry on.

B: So you wrap your leash round your fingers so Kes is now fastened to your hand. When you've reached this stage and he's feeding from your hand regular and not bating too much …

MF: Bating … what's that?

B: Trying to fly off, in a panic like. So now you can try feeding him outside and getting him used to things.

Activity 2

a
i In this extract Billy uses some specialist language to explain his hobby, such as 'jesses'. What other specialist words does he use?

ii Look carefully at the moments when Billy uses a new jargon word. Describe what tends to happen straight after he uses these technical terms for the first time.

Think about the pattern in the language you have identified. Discuss and/or write down the possible reasons for the pattern.

b

c What are the advantages and disadvantages of Billy using jargon in this situation? Think about it from the perspectives of the different individuals involved: Billy, Mr Farthing, and the rest of the class.

The following transcript is of an interview between Mike, a bank manager, and Owen, a man who is hoping to get a loan to start up a new business. Mike is questioning Owen's business proposal for a mothers' online networking and advisory service.

Mike: how many (.) mothers have you (.) spoken to to verify that they would **sign up** for (.) this advice service

Owen: direct (.) erm (.) correspondence on this (.) is time-consuming is labour-intensive //and//

Mike: //so// my question is (.) how many mothers of young children have you spoken to (.) about their **willingness** to actually **pay for** a new mothers' service

Owen: the proposal has been informed by my partner (.) in the local area the numbers in this demographic are **strong** and the projected uptake of this service will be very high (.) on //a national scale//

Mike: //how many//

Owen: the demand for e-subscription will be even better

Mike: so I just need numbers here

Owen: (1) I haven't confirmed the exact properties of the service to the target consumer

Mike: so you haven't spoken to any mothers

Owen: **not** for this particular service

Mike: what you're doing is you're asking for investment of fifty thousand pounds but what you're saying is I **haven't** done the market research **required**

Owen: yes the design process has been the focus and I haven't asked the question (.) will you subscribe to e-Mums but (.) I think it's obvious at this stage that the design is the the key unique selling point

Activity 3

a Here Owen attempts to avoid answering the initial question. Why doesn't he give a straight answer?

b What tactics does Owen use to try to make himself and his business idea seem more convincing? Copy and complete the table below.

Describe the tactic he uses and give an example.	Explain what you think he hopes the effect will be.
He uses several long, complex words.	*He hopes these word choices will make him sound more intelligent and that the bank manager will take him more seriously.*

c Imagine you are the business investor. Write a short reference, summarising your experience of interviewing Owen and explaining whether or not you think he could be worthy of investment.

Street talk

Most of us adapt our language depending on the situation we are in. If we are talking to someone we do not know very well, or someone who we think has a higher status than us, we might be more careful, more polite and more **formal** in our speech.

However, when we are in private, with people we know well, we loosen up in our language use, using more informal words, expressions and less carefully thought-out sentences and pronunciation.

So just as you would probably avoid greeting your Head of Year 'All right mate?', it is also unlikely you would ask your little brother to 'Kindly refrain from making that irritating noise'. We know, often without even thinking, what words are best to use in different situations. In general though, spoken language tends to be less formal in its **register** than written language.

When analysing spoken language, there are different ways we can describe the informal expressions we hear being used. You might describe someone as talking in a colloquial way (or using colloquialisms), which means they are using informal, chatty language that anyone can understand. Colloquial language can often sound very casual and familiar.

When talking in this way some people also use **slang**. Like jargon, slang is a bit more specialist: only certain groups of people use and understand it. Slang can change from generation to generation and fall in and out of fashion with different groups at different times.

These texts and activities will help you to understand why people use slang and the different effects it can have.

> ## Key terms
>
> **Formal:** describes language that is polite, official or complex.
>
> **Register:** the style of language used in a particular context; language can have a formal, informal or mixed register.
>
> **Slang:** very informal words and phrases that are used and understood by only certain groups of people.

Think about how rap artists like Plan B use street talk to convey their message

Speaking and listening

Work with a partner. Look at the utterances in the list below. Discuss whether you would class the words used in each instance as 'colloquial', 'slang' or 'jargon'.

'Hey, how you doing?'

'We need to set out the foundations along the line of the boundary.'

'That sucks, you must be hacked off.'

'We'll be teeing off for a par 4 but take into account the dog-leg on the right.'

'The film was wicked man, you should try to catch it.'

'We had a great time on our hols.'

> The following transcript is from an online radio review show featuring two presenters called Lennie and Monique.

Lennie: alright so listen right something else that **we** like to do on this show is letting people know what is **hot** and what **ain't** ok **swag** we're talking about **swag**

Monique: now obviously you can see Len's in the denim swag

Lennie: and Monique she is **rockin** the red today (.) that's swagalicious right there (.)

Monique: [laughing] ok but there are people we feel need to **update** their swag

Lennie: that's right (.) check out the swag **doctor** and **fix** that illness right so first up (2) Plan B man (.) **really** how many grey suits you got man (.) come on man you look like you been locked out in the rain man (.) **fix up** man put on a hoodie

Monique: you might think we're being a bit harsh but we're gonna go the other way and big up the people who **have** got swag ok

Lennie: oh there's bare people who've got swag (.) right take a look at this

Monique: yes Tinie **Tempah** (.) different **kind** of swag

Lennie: (.) that guy (.) **that's** how you wear a suit man (.) I am feelin that (.) that's how you wear suits Plan B now fix up man

Activity 1

a Match the slang used by Lennie and Monique (on the left) to the definitions (on the right). Remember to look back at the transcript. It may help you to work out what some of the words mean by looking at how the speakers use them.

A	hot	a	show support for
B	*swag*	b	lots of
C	*check out*	c	in trend or fashionable
D	*fix up*	d	look at or go and see something
E	*hoodie*	e	someone's style or appearance
F	*harsh*	f	a hooded sweatshirt
G	*big up*	g	to make improvements
H	*bare*	h	cruel or unfair

b Lennie uses the adjective 'swagalicious' to describe his own clothes. He may have invented this word but what do you think it means? Try to give a reason for your answer.

c You might not use the same slang words as Lennie and Monique. People of different ages and from different regions often use different slang. What slang words would you use to mean the following?

- good
- bad
- to run away
- to feel tired
- to miss school without permission
- to tell on someone

Stretch yourself

You could investigate the slang used in your area by doing a survey. Ask people from a range of age groups what words they use. Do people of the same age use similar words? Look for similarities and patterns in the data you collect.

The following extract is from a play called *Our Day Out*. In the play, a class of secondary school children are taken out on a day trip.

As the coach goes along the city streets the kids are talking and laughing and pointing. On the back seat, Reilly secretly takes out a packet of cigarettes. The little kid sees them.

Digga: Reilly, light up.

Reilly: Where's Briggsy?

Digga: He's at the front, I'll keep dixie. Come on we're all right, light up.

Little Kid: Agh 'ey. You've got ciggies. I'm gonna tell miss.

Reilly: Shut up you an' open that friggin' window.

Little Kid: No ... I'm gonna tell miss.

Digga: Go'n tell her. She won't do nott'n anyway.

Little Kid: I'll tell sir.

Reilly: You do an' I'll gob y'.

Digga: Come on ... open that window, you.

Little Kid: Why?

Reilly: Why d' y' think? So we get a bit of fresh air.

Little Kid: Well there's no fresh air round here. You just wanna smoke. An' smokin' stunts y' growth.

Reilly: I'll stunt your friggin' growth if y' don't get it open.

Activity 2

a All three characters in this extract speak in a colloquial way but we form different opinions of them based on what they say and how they say it. Which stereotype do you think best describes the characters? Tick the boxes you think apply to the characters.

	Digga	Reilly	Little Kid
The victim			✓
The accomplice			
The goody two shoes			
The bully			
The sneak			
The bad boy			

b Reilly and Digga seem to use more slang words and phrases than Little Kid. Look carefully at the examples below. What do these expressions tell us about the character?

Slang	Explain what this choice of language shows about the character
Digga: 'I'll keep Dixie.'	*Digga is willing to keep watch for Reilly. Maybe he is just be being a good friend, or he might be too scared of getting caught himself to take the lead.*
Reilly: 'open that friggin' window.'	
Reilly: 'I'll go by'.'	

c It is not unusual for 'bad' characters to use slang in books, plays, TV and films. Some people look down on slang as not being 'proper' English, but slang does have its uses. For example, when a radio or TV programme is trying to appeal to a young audience, the presenters often use the slang of that age group to make the show more appealing to them. Try to think of two more situations when using slang might have some advantages.

Individual groups like the Black Rebel Motorcycle Club have their own slang particular to their generation

Each generation has its own slang. You might not think it, but people of all ages will probably have had their own informal expressions for things just as you do.

The following transcript is from a 1950s film, *The Wild One*. The film is about two rival motorcycle gangs. In this extract Johnny, the young leader of the Black Rebel Motorcycle Club, has arrived in a new town and is talking to Kathie, a local waitress.

Kathie: What do you do (1) I mean do you just ride around or do you go on some sort of a picnic or something?

Johnny: A picnic? man you are too square I, I, I'm' a have to straighten you out (1) now listen you don't go any one special place that's cornball style (.) you just go (1) a bunch get together after all week and it builds up (.) you just (.) the idea is to just have a ball (.) now if you're going to stay cool you've got to wail (.) you've got to put something down you've got to make some jive don't you know what I'm talking about?

Kathie: Yeah yeah, I know what you mean.

Activity 3

a Johnny seems to be disappointed in Kathie's questions. Choose a quote that you think shows his negative attitude and explain what you think he means.

b Johnny speaks more than Kathie and he also uses a lot of slang. Look at the following possible reasons for his use of slang. Number the reasons in this list from 1 to 6 according to how much you think they will influence Johnny's use of slang. 1 = very likely to influence him, 6 = least likely to influence him.

- They are in a café.
- He is in a motorcycle gang.
- He is a young man.
- He is trying to impress Kathie.
- He is from out of town.
- He has got into the habit of using slang.

If you are working with others, compare your lists and discuss any differences in your choices.

c The paragraph below explains why one of the factors listed above might be important. Look closely at the way the paragraph is structured.

Johnny may be using slang because he is in a gang. He uses lots of slang words like 'wail' and 'jive' to describe how he and his friends in the gang spend their time. People in a gang often want to exclude outsiders and so they invent words to use between themselves that no one else will understand.

A clear point is made about Johnny's use of slang.

Some examples of the slang he uses are given.

The point is developed and explained further.

Now try to write your own explanation, exploring a different reason for Johnny's use of slang. In your explanation, use some examples from the transcript.

Loaded words

Words are pretty powerful things. A single word can trigger all sorts of reactions in people. Take the word 'skeleton', for example.

When you see this word, you might think of secrets, ghosts and dark places. Or you might think of history, dinosaurs and digging up the ground. Or you might even think of science, X-rays and body parts.

Writers often use the associations (or connotations) of particular words to get a specific response from their reading audience.

But it is not just writers who choose their words carefully for the effects they have and the meanings they create. In spoken language, we do the same thing. When we want to express a certain emotion or feeling, or when we want our listener to react in a certain way, then these words can be described as **emotive**.

These texts and activities show you how opinion and emotion can be expressed through people's word choices and how their choices can influence the person they are speaking to.

The following transcript is from an interview with a music artist outside an award ceremony. He has been asked to explain why music matters to him.

> **Key term**
>
> **Emotive:** describes a word or phrase that provokes a strong emotional response in the audience.

Music matters to me because it was the one thing that gave me like a a passion a dream a hunger something to really live for you know I think at the end of the day (.) everybody can sort of wake up and get on with their ordinary life but discovering music and falling in love with it made me realise that (.) I had a purpose I had something that I wanted to do and I had something that I had to work my butt off to achieve you know and that's why music matters to me.

Activity 1

a In your own words sum up how this person feels about making music.

b Choose two phrases from the musician's answer which you think have the most positive connotations.

c When speaking persuasively or enthusiastically, people often use triples to emphasise their points. What list of three does the music artist use to emphasise the positive effect that music has had on him?

Speaking and listening

> **Key terms**
>
> **Denotation:** the literal, dictionary meaning of a word. This is often different to the connotations the word may have.
>
> **Implied meaning:** meaning is suggested rather than being direct and obvious.

Sometimes the literal meaning of a word, its **denotation**, can be different to its **implied meaning** (connotation). Work with a partner. Discuss the list of words below which, on the surface, mean very similar things. What are the connotations of each word? Are some more positive or negative than others? Do some of the words make you think of certain things that the others don't?

- child
- tot
- kid
- youngster
- infant
- minor

The following transcript is from an interview that took place during a well-publicised government inquiry into press standards. In this transcript, the actor Hugh Grant is giving his view of the British press.

I **just** think that there has been (.) a **section** of our press that has become – **allowed** to become toxic over the last 20 or 30 years (.) er its main tactic being bullying and intimidation and blackmail (.) and I think that that needs a lot of **courage** to stand up to and I feel that it's time (.) you know this country has had historically a good record standing up to bullies and I think it's time that this country found the courage to stand up to this bully now.

Activity 2

a Hugh Grant is clearly very concerned about British newspapers, describing the press as 'toxic'. The denotation of 'toxic' is 'poisonous', but what connotations does this word have? Why do you think Hugh Grant has chosen this word?

b He is trying to encourage the people at the inquiry and the TV audience to share his view of the press. He chooses his words carefully in order to try to create an emotional response in the listener. Where does he do this?

Short quote where emotive language is used	How are we supposed to feel?

c Hugh Grant changes his word choice in the opening line when he says 'has become – allowed to become'. What has he suggested by rephrasing his utterance in this way?

The following transcript is from a discussion that took place on a live TV show about football. In this transcript, the panel of presenters are commenting on an incident involving a Premier League player.

Jeff: of course the other headline that came out of Chelsea this week was that Ashley Cole (1) brought an air rifle to training and **shot** a student [sighs] what was he thinking of

Alan: I couldn't tell you Jeff (.) it's the **stupidest** thing I've heard (1) in twenty years of football […]

Charlie: I've heard some (.) absolutely ridiculous stuff (.) but I've never heard of anything as (.) way out as wacky as this

Matt: it's bizarre (.) it's bizarre really unbelievable

Jeff describes the incident by saying Ashley Cole 'brought an air rifle to training and shot a student'. He uses the word 'shot', a short, emotive word on which he puts added stress.

Activity 3

a Evaluate the following alternatives and explain whether they are better or worse options. Remember to think about whether the meaning, register and effect are appropriate for the context.

Ashley Cole brought an air rifle to training and:

- hit a student
- popped a cap in a student
- fired at a student.

b The three panellists Alan, Charlie and Matt seem in agreement in terms of their attitude. However, they use different language techniques to emphasise how they feel. For each technique listed below, try to find an example.

- Using emotive words
- Exaggerating
- Putting added stress on a word
- Listing
- Using repetition

c People in the media often use exaggerated forms of language as the commentators have done here. In particular you hear this when news stories are reported on radio and TV. Why is this? What effect might these language choices have on the audience?

Check your learning

In this unit you have learned some new terminology to describe the word choices people make in their speech.

Test yourself

What do the following terms mean?

- Jargon
- Colloquial
- Slang
- Adjective
- Emotive
- Connotations
- Denotation

You have also learned about some of the situations where particular types of words are commonly found.

Test yourself

Look at the list of contexts below. In a copy of the table, for each one explain what type of language you would be most likely to hear:

- jargon
- colloquialisms/slang
- emotive language.

Context	Type of language and why
Friends chatting	
A speech from a political leader	
Radio 1 music show	
Doctor's consultation room	
Sports commentary	
Documentary on the natural world	

Grammar and structure: Stories, texts and tweets

Spoken language is often structured and organised in different ways to written language. There are lots of different reasons for this. One of the key reasons is that spoken language tends to be used when talking in real time and face to face with other people. It is not usually as planned as written language, so this can mean that its structures are more flexible. For example, we can adapt what we say depending on what reactions we get from other people, such as:

- their facial expressions
- their body language
- the replies they might give
- what is going on around us.

We can use different structures and types of expression to do different jobs in different circumstances, such as checking to see if people are listening, giving instructions and explaining or describing events that have taken place.

As you will see from the work you do later in this unit, this is one of the more challenging parts of spoken language study and you will probably need to make a few notes about some of the technical terms along the way. Keep a note of the new terms you pick up and then check your learning at the end of the unit. These are not just labels for the sake of labels, but useful and precise terms that can be applied to particular features of speech. In fact, by the time you get to the section on **vague language** you will probably realise why we need to be quite precise when using language in some situations.

An annotated example

In the following example a gym instructor is introducing new students to the facilities on offer. His **primary purpose** is to explain how to use the gym equipment and why it is important not to just go straight in and start exercising. His **secondary purpose** is to make sure that the students understand what he has said and that they are paying attention. His choices of grammar and structure are, therefore, closely linked to these purposes.

The transcript below has been annotated to give you guidance about the kinds of features to look out for and how they help create meaning.

Key terms

Vague language: expressions typical in speech which are often used to finish utterances or to make the speaker sound less certain.

Primary purpose: the main aim of what you are trying to communicate.

Secondary purpose: other aims you might have.

Statements (declaratives): utterances or clauses that state a point (rather than asking a question or giving a command).

Instructor: all right guys (.) welcome to the erm (.) college fitness suite (2) before we start the induction (1) we'll be running through some basics about how to sign in at the desk (.)

The instructor explains here what will be involved before the induction starts. He is using **statements (declaratives)** to inform his audience of what will be happening.

then it will basically be us (.) taking a look at all the equipment (1) pointing out the safety implications of err each piece of equipment and making sure that you can use it all

He goes on to use three **dynamic verbs** here which give a clear sense of the different parts of the induction. There is a form of structure here which is called **cohesion**. Similar types of words are used in similar ways to explain a clear pattern to what is going to take place.

(Continues overleaf)

45

The instructor uses the **conjunctions** 'so' and 'and' to link together different parts of what he has said and give a clear reason for what they are doing.

correctly (.) so that when you come to work out for the first time (.) you know what you are doing and you're not gonna cause injury to yourself or others (.)

He uses a clear **signposting device** here to structure what he is saying. By numbering or listing what he is going to explain, he helps the listeners understand and take in the information.

What I'll get you to do after we've finished is (.) to look at the rules and regulations (.) the type of things we'll expect from you (.) and err one of those err things will be about making sure you bring your ID card with you each time (1) another thing will be about telling us about any injuries or health problems you've got

Here the instructor uses a question (interrogative) to check if his audience are listening and they show that they understand by nodding.

So, I hope that makes sense (.) is that clear?

Students: [respond by nodding]

He uses **directives** in his speech to the students to give clear instructions. These take the form of **imperatives** like 'check' and 'adjust', or **modal verbs** (like 'must' and 'should') that exert a degree of pressure on the listeners to do what he says.

Instructor: The first thing I need to stress is that you must use the equipment in the way it's intended (1) you can injure yourself quite badly (.) and damage the equipment if you don't do it properly (1) so you should always do the following (.) on this running machine check the settings first (.) adjust to your stride if necessary (.) like this and then find the right pace

Speech often makes use of references to things around us. If we are talking to people who can all see the things that we can see we often 'point' towards them with particular words, like 'this', 'that' and 'here'. These are called deictic words because they point to words in the immediate environment.

Once you've found the right speed you can adjust the speed up or down like this (1) but don't go too high too quickly or you'll end up **whoah** (.) flat on your face like that (.) so take it gently yeah (.) and you can set the timer here for either how many kilometres you want to run (.) so like 5k 10k whatever (.) or for how long you want to run (.) ten minutes twenty minutes OK

Later in the transcript, after the instructor has been through all the equipment and safety issues, he rounds everything off.

So, that's pretty much it I hope that's been of use to you (1) any questions please ask me (.) OK guys thanks very much

Spoken language does not always make use of full sentences: it does not really need to because it is not written down and we can 'punctuate' our language in other ways. It is clear what the instructor means and there is no confusion.

Here the instructor rounds off what he is saying by moving back to the friendly style he used at the beginning, signalling that he has finished the serious bit and is finishing off his talk.

Structures in spoken and written language

Speech and writing often do very different jobs. When you think about it, you probably do much more of your communication every day in speech than you do in writing. And when you first look at a transcript you might – like lots of people – say that it looks broken up, unstructured, full of hesitations and that it is not 'proper English'. As you study spoken English more closely, you will probably change your mind about these things. For a start, spoken language has lots of structure to it. It is usually organised into units of meaning and those units of meaning are linked together in various ways, but the way we do this is often different to how we would do it in writing.

One feature that is common to the structure of spoken language is **ellipsis**. This is when the speaker leaves out whole words, phrases or even longer chunks of language. This usually happens because they are not needed in the context and can be filled in by a mixture of common sense and awareness of what has already been said and who is talking.

In the transcripts and extracts that follow, we will look at ways in which speech can be structured and think about the similarities and differences between this and writing. One of the first areas we will look at is how spoken language often leaves gaps that we would not see in written language.

The following extract is taken from a conversation between a customer and a sales assistant in a shop.

C: two of the number 8 scratch cards please and a book of stamps

SA: first or second class

C: first please

SA: 6 or 12

C: err (.) 6 please

SA: anything else

C: no that's great thanks

The second transcript is taken from a storybook for young children about a girl on holiday.

Jane didn't have much of her holiday money left and wondered if she'd have enough for an ice cream. The ice cream man served the children in front of her and then turned to her.

'What would you like then, my dear?'

(Continues overleaf)

Key terms

Dynamic verbs: verbs that describe physical actions.

Cohesion: the way that a text or piece of speech holds together through features such as repeated words and structures.

Conjunctions: words used to link together other words, phrases or clauses (e.g. 'and', 'but', 'if').

Signposting device: a word or phrase used to help listeners follow the structure of what is being said.

Directive: a sentence or utterance acting as a kind of command or order.

Imperative: a sentence that acts as a command.

Modal verb: a type of verb that works with a main verb to add a degree of certainty, obligation or doubt.

Confirmation checks: words and phrases used to check if the listener is following.

Ellipsis: missing out words, phrases or larger clause elements.

'How much are the large cones, please,' she asked.

'They're one pound fifty,' he replied.

That was too much. She only had about one pound twenty left.

'Oh, how much are the small cones then?'

'They're one pound thirty.'

Jane counted out her coins, but it wasn't enough.

'How much have you got there?' asked the man.

'I've got one pound twenty five,' Jane replied sadly.

'That'll do. Just give us that,' said the man and he served her an ice cream.

'Thank you,' said Jane.

Activity 1

a What do you think is the main difference between the real speech in the first extract and the written speech in the second extract?

b In the table below you can see three extracts from the first transcript. Think about how each of these would be turned into full sentences in written **Standard English** and write your version in the right-hand column.

Shortened version	Full version
Two of the number 8 scratchcards please and a book of stamps	Please may I have two of the number 8 scratchcards and a book of stamps
First or second class	
First please	

c Now read through the second extract and think about how you could make this sound more like real speech. Complete a table like the one below, using the same sort of ellipsis that we have just seen in the first extract and in the modelled transcript at the start of this unit.

Full version	Shortened version
'They're one pound fifty,' he replied.	One pound fifty

As well as ellipsis, spoken language often consists of vague language. This is usually in the form of clusters of words that go together as units, such as 'you know', 'if you see what I mean', 'and everything' and 'or something'. Vague language is much more common in speech than in writing and can be used in many different ways. One important function of vague language is to soften what is said or make it sound less certain.

Activity 2

a Work with a partner. Discuss the expressions below and rank them in order of how certain they sound, with the most certain at the top and the least certain at the bottom.

   i   At about lunchtime

   ii At precisely 1.30pm

   iii At one-ish

   iv Later today, or something

   v At half past one, or near enough

b Looking at the expressions above, pick out the words and phrases that you think might be classed as **vague language**. Why are they vague?

c Now have a look at the extracts of language below. Imagine you are trying to be as vague or non-committal as possible. Discuss and then rewrite each to sound much less certain.

Certain	Vague
18,997 people went to the game.	*About 20,000 people went to the game.*
I will see you at 8.45pm, exactly 24 hours from now.	
A group of 6 men caused £15,550 damage to the bus.	
I'd like three 1 litre bottles of the sugar-free cola drink flavoured with vegetable extract.	
Can you get me a sandwich, baguette, roll or wrap, please?	

Review and reflect

Above we have looked at examples of vague language in speech, but not really asked **why** people often prefer to be vague when they speak.

a What benefits might there be of using vague language? Think about how you appear to other people if you use very precise and detailed language all the time. What impression do you think they might have of you? Too sure? Too assertive? Perhaps a little bit cocky?

b Think of people, perhaps in particular occupations, who need to use precise language – why do you think they do so?

c There are lots of good reasons to use vague language and many of these are to do with how we present a 'face' to other people in speech. Can you think of situations when you would be deliberately vague and why you might choose to be like this?

As well as vague language, another kind of feature that we often add in spoken language is what is called the **quotative**. This is a really common feature that nearly everyone uses when they explain what someone has said or thought and how they said it.

> **Key term**
>
> **Quotative:** an expression used to describe the way in which someone said something.

A: I bet she was in a right state

B: it wasn't a lot of fun (.) she was really upset so I said to her come on it's only a phone (.) we can phone up the company and block it and then get you another one on the insurance

A: ah right

B: and she was all right after that (.) I think she was worried it'd be a big problem with the bill or whatever

For example, in the following transcript you can see that 'So I said to her' is used to explain what speaker B said to her daughter when she was upset about her phone being stolen.

There are lots of different types of quotatives, and some differences between how people of different ages use them. The transcript below is taken from a teenager's account of an incident at his school.

Zack: no it was like (.) it was the end of school yeah so that school's finished yeah and everyone was going home and I was getting my bike from the bike rack and I was going out and I was riding my bike and he stopped my bike (1) I was like 'yeah' and he goes 'get off the bike' I was like 'why am I getting off the bike I'm going home like I've gotta go home' yeah he was like 'no get off the bike walk the bike outside of school' I was like 'what's the point' yeah cos like it's quite far like to get out the school from the entrance like in the school yeah and he goes 'ah no get off the bike' yeah so like he kind of shoved me off the bike so I dropped it but I didn't fall over like but I kind of stumbled yeah and he put his (.) he tried to take my bike up to his office like he was gonna keep my bike there (.) I was like 'no'

Activity 3

a Make a copy of Zack's statement. Try to ring the seven quotatives used in the transcript. Check your answers with a partner before moving on. Have you got them all?

b Think of other quotatives that could have been used instead. Replace the seven quotatives with three or four different ones.

c When you think about your own language use, which quotatives do you tend to use most? Give them one tick for occasional use or if you hear others around you using them, two ticks for the most frequently used and a cross if you do not use them at all:

I said	I was
I was like	I says
This is me	I told him/her

Think about the age of this speaker. He is a teenager, but would you expect an older person to use quotatives in the same way? Discuss with a partner how you might work out what different quotatives are used by different age groups. Have a look at the list of them above and see if you can work out which ones your grandparents and parents might be most likely to use. Some people have very strong – often quite negative – views about how young people talk. When you look at the attitudes unit in this book (Unit 7) you will find some examples of media texts where writers and commentators describe young people's speech as 'inarticulate' or 'lazy'. How fair are such views do you think?

Telling stories

So far, you have looked at things that get left out in speech (ellipsis) and things that are inserted in speech (vague language).

Now we will look at how ideas are organised and how structure is maintained in speech. In written language, we are used to seeing:

- punctuation
- paragraphing
- sentences.

We do not have those in spoken language, but there are many different ways of organising what we say.

Read the extract of a transcript below, which is taken from a college principal greeting new students and telling them what they will be doing at their new college. Think about how the principal signposts what she is telling the students. Signposting is an effective way of signalling to your listeners what you will be telling them about in detail later on, and showing them that you are moving from one idea to another. For example, a speaker might use a word like 'furthermore' or a phrase like 'on the other hand' to signal that they are about to move on or add a contrasting point.

P: Hello and welcome to all of you (2) this morning I will be telling you a little bit about what you can expect in the year to come (.) some of the expectations we have of you (.) what you can expect from us (1) I will be introducing you to some of the faces you will be seeing around college during your first few days with us (.) and telling you about some of the things you will need to do over this first induction week (2) but first (.) let me just say how pleased I am that you have chosen Fulchester College to continue your studies and what a wise choice you have made

Activity 1

a Identify which signposting techniques the speaker has used to structure her speech.

b Which words and phrases has she used to help her organise her ideas clearly?

c Why is it important for her to signpost and signal what she is about to tell the students in this situation?

Can you think of other ways in which speakers signpost what they are talking about? Look back over the transcript at the start of this unit and also think about talks that you have been given at school, college or at work. Make a note of the different signposting techniques used by these speakers.

Another way of structuring speech is to use **discourse markers**, which are devices that draw our attention to the fact that something new or something important is about to be said. These are often single words like 'so' and 'right', which are frequently used at the start of a new topic, but they can also be words like 'and' and 'but' that are used to link topics together and show connections between what has been said before.

P: so your research tells us that there is no direct link between video games and violent behaviour (.) is that about it basically

V: well it's a very complicated picture (.) in fact some research carried out last year seemed to suggest that in a few cases (.) where young people had been playing what might be classed as violent games for at least six to eight hours a day (.) quite extreme cases it has to be said (.) there was an increase in aggressive behaviour (.) however our latest research suggests that it's a murkier picture

Activity 2

a   Identify the four discourse markers in the transcript. It is taken from a radio interview between a presenter (P) and a video games expert (V).

b   Which of these discourse markers help to introduce a new idea and which link back to something that has gone before?

c   Have a look back at the gym instruction extract at the start of this unit. Try to identify the discourse markers being used by the instructor and how they are being used.

i   Are discourse markers used to link ideas together or to show contrast between them?

ii   Are any being used to kick off a new topic or draw the attention of the audience?

Spoken language is often used to tell stories or recount events that have taken place. Another way of structuring spoken language to do this type of job is to follow particular patterns that make it easier for listeners to understand the order in which events took place and where they fit into the overall picture. Most narratives like this fit into a simple structure along the lines of:

Scene setting: details such as where, when and who was involved

↓

Event: something takes place leading to a conclusion

↓

Reaction: some view is expressed about what has happened

Activity 3

a The transcript below is taken from an eyewitness account of an anti-cuts demonstration in London. Can you identify which parts of the transcript fit into the scene-setting, event and reaction parts of the narrative structure?

Basically err (.) I was at Tower Hill tube with Paul (.) err waiting for Gary and Rashid to get there (.) there was like hundreds of people (.) all with placards and banners (.) people were meeting up with their mates (1) I could hear police horses coming closer and then this guy near me shouted they're charging they're charging and it was like **whoa** (.) looked round and there was four or five mounted police bombing towards us (.) we just dived out of the way into this newsagents' doorway and they just like swept by (1) don't think I've ever come that close to getting trampled before

b In the transcript, the speaker begins by using the past tense ('I was …'). What do you notice about the way that other past tense and present tense verbs are used in this account? Where can you see verbs describing actions in the past tense and where can you see verbs in the present tense?

c When you look at the way in which the speaker makes this sound dramatic, which word choices are particularly important?

Stretch yourself

Narratives are very common in spoken language and provide really good data for you to analyse. Think about ways in which you can record your own short narratives from people you know.

- Record different family members telling you about the most embarrassing moment in their lives.
- Ask friends to tell you about their first day at school.
- If you record several different people doing the same thing, you can then think about how different types of people (younger/older, male/female, family members/friends) tell stories in particular ways.

This is the sort of data that can really help you when you are being assessed on your understanding of how different people use spoken language.

Multimodal texts

Nearly all of the material you have studied so far in this book consists of genuinely spoken language, but there are relatively new forms of communication that use some aspects of spoken language even though they are not actually spoken.

Think about the language that you might use in a Facebook conversation, on Twitter or when sending texts on your phone. These are all forms of **computer-mediated communication (CMC)**, which use some elements of the structure and grammar of spoken language. This is often because online communication involves the sort of interaction that is similar to spoken language.

For example, when we text or chat online, we expect to get some sort of reply, which means that we take turns (like in speech), we often share an understanding of what it is we're talking about, and we want to communicate fairly quickly, so the emphasis is often on making a point rather than producing 'perfect' language.

Have a look at Example 1 below. This is an example of a tweet – a Twitter message – sent by a user to his timeline.

Compared to how this would be written in Standard English, there are some features that are different.

We can still read this message and understand it, assuming we know a bit about football and know what the message was referring to. And while the grammar is a bit **compressed**, it is still clear. For example, we do not really need 'I' at the start of the first sentence, because if we are reading this tweet we know who has sent it.

Writers using CMC forms like this are not always thinking of grammatical accuracy as their first priority when they are sending messages. They are probably more interested in getting their message sent as quickly as possible, so some of the features we see are due to that.

As well as using a compressed style of grammar, users of CMC tend to abbreviate more regularly than in more formal writing. For example, numbers and letters can be swapped for words or parts of words:

- '8' for 'ate or eight'
- '2' for 'to' or 'too'
- 'U' for 'you', and so on.

You would expect a written message to include a subject (e.g. 'I wonder'.)

You would expect a name of a place to be capitalised.

Unless it is actually a question, you would probably not use a question mark for a statement like this person has.

The hashtag # is also an interesting feature of this form of communication. It allows people to look for tweets about that topic (in this case Leeds United FC #LUFC) to see what someone else has said.

Abbreviation can also involve cutting out parts of words so we often see vowels missed out because we can read words quite well 'wtht thm'.

As well as shortening sentences and cutting down words, many CMC forms add extra bits of punctuation too. When we are speaking to each other we can tell a lot about how the other person feels from many of the following:

- how quickly they speak
- their **intonation** (how the voice goes up and down)
- the emphasis they put on certain words or sounds within words
- their facial expressions (smiling, looking as if they are joking, looking serious).

With many CMC forms we do not get to see the other person's face or hear their voice, so punctuation and symbols are used to add those tones and hints. So, we often see multiple punctuation marks like '???' or smileys and other **emoticons** such as the following:

Jon Cooper @coopzinnit   15m

RT @lufcbarmyarmy: Soooo want to believe this!!!! #LUFC

www.guardian.co.uk/football/takeover

Details

Wesley Headley @westheledge   27m

I cant take this no more !!!!
On... off... done... collapsed?
Arghhhh!! Sort it out KB!
#Pen4Ken #lufc #BatesOut

Details

What u doin goin out with him???
Only joking :-O

When is game on? Need to know so can sort lift out

Activity 1

Have a look at the tweets and texts.

a Write out any examples of abbreviations and compressed grammar that have been used in one colour.

b Write out any examples of extra punctuation and emoticons in another colour.

c What extra meanings or intentions do you think might be conveyed by the extra punctuation and emoticons? Try to explain what difference they might make to the messages and how they should be read.

Not everyone uses abbreviations – and predictive text and smartphones often fill in whole words or phrases automatically now – but they are still fairly common in many messages.

Activity 2

a Read and think about the following texts, which are taken from messages sent by teenagers to friends. Rank the messages in order. Put the messages that are most compressed and abbreviated at one end and the least compressed and abbreviated at the other.

> Hey you ok? Heard you weren't feelin well …

> I'm so sorry, i no it mite jus b wrds but im really sori 4 2day

> If I don't remember to call you, flash me after 4.30pm. Carla.

> Leanne babe quik question do u think frm wen u last saw me i have put on weight? Txt bk asap xax

b Now try to work out what kind of abbreviation or compression has been used in each message. Which words or parts of words have been missed out? See if you can fill in what the Standard English version might look like.

Compressed version	Standard English version
Hey you ok? Heard you weren't feelin well …	*Hey are you OK? I heard that you were not feeling well.*
I'm so sorry, i no it mite jus b wrds but im really sori 4 2day	
If I don't remember to call you, flash me after 4.30pm. Carla.	
Leanne babe quik question do u think frm wen u last saw me i have put on weight? Txt bk asap xax	

c Now think about some of the messages on your phone – or via other forms of CMC such as internet chat or online forums – that you have sent or received in the past few days. Do these messages follow a similar pattern? Write a few of them out and see if you can spot the same features.

Stretch yourself

If you think about your own style of language, you might notice that it has changed as you have got older. When you were three or four you probably could not write properly at all, but by the time you were seven or eight you will have been writing in sentences and spelling most basic words correctly.

Now you are older, you will probably notice that your texting style has changed too. One good way of looking at changes over time is to compare the texting style of four or five different people of different ages. See if you can come up with a way of doing this so you can see if there is a marked difference between how a 12-year-old child texts compared to one of your friends or one of your parents.

Now think about some of the following types of CMC: emails, Facebook messages and online chat. These forms often have longer, more detailed conversations. Emails too can often have great importance in the workplace where they are used to communicate more formally and are often written in a more traditionally formal style, although this does vary from place to place and person to person.

One important point about all of these forms of communication is that we all have our own styles of communicating when we use them – just like in speech – so when looking at conversations between different people, you should make sure you look at individual differences and not just the features of that particular type of technology.

The extract below is taken from an online forum where music fans discuss their favourite performers at a festival.

Activity 3

a Identify examples of the following in the conversation:

i ellipsis

ii abbreviation

iii emoticons

iv extra punctuation

v other examples of non-standard language.

b Can you identify any differences in the ways the individual posters use grammar and structure?

c Why do you think there are differences in the posters' individual styles?

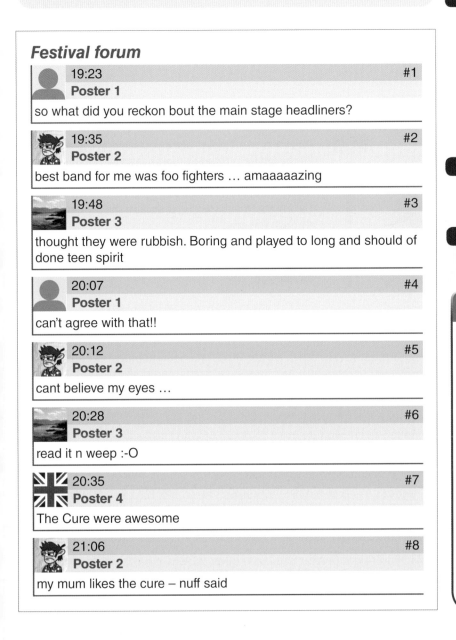

Festival forum

19:23   #1
Poster 1

so what did you reckon bout the main stage headliners?

19:35   #2
Poster 2

best band for me was foo fighters … amaaaaazing

19:48   #3
Poster 3

thought they were rubbish. Boring and played to long and should of done teen spirit

20:07   #4
Poster 1

can't agree with that!!

20:12   #5
Poster 2

cant believe my eyes …

20:28   #6
Poster 3

read it n weep :-O

20:35   #7
Poster 4

The Cure were awesome

21:06   #8
Poster 2

my mum likes the cure – nuff said

Check your learning

In this unit you have looked at:

- differences and similarities between the structure of spoken and written language
- how spoken language signposts key ideas
- how narratives can be structured in speech
- some of the ways in which spoken language leaves words and phrases out (ellipsis), adds extra bits (vague language and quotatives)
- how CMC uses elements from both spoken and written language
- how individuals use different types of structure and style.

5

Planned and unplanned speech: The right words at the right time

Spoken language comes in all sorts of forms and happens in all sorts of situations. If you think about all the different times you speak and hear others speaking in a normal week, there will be hundreds, maybe thousands, of different ways in which speech is used.

For example, there are:

- casual conversations with friends on the bus or walking to school
- conversations with members of your family
- chats on the phone
- people talking on the radio
- teachers talking to classes at school
- students talking to whole year groups in school assemblies.

Speaking and listening

a Work in a small group. See if you can draw up a list of all the different types of spoken language you hear in a normal day. You might want to log it all and make a quick note of who was talking, what they were talking about and then refer back to this as you go through this unit.

b Alternatively, take a normal hour at school and make a note of all the different types of talk you hear around you.

One thing that we might notice about speech is that it can vary in its degree of planning. A huge amount of speech is spontaneous and unplanned. In other words, it has not been planned out and rehearsed beforehand, but comes out at that moment. You will probably have noticed that even though some speech is unplanned it does have a certain structure to it. For instance, if we are buying a train ticket or asking directions from someone, things normally happen as we would expect in terms of who speaks when and the kinds of things that are said.

That is because even unplanned speech normally follows a **scheme**. And even when you are chatting to friends, however everyday the subject matter – yesterday's football transfers, who you saw on the way home, the colour of your socks, your mate's rubbish ringtone – speech tends to follow basic rules and meet certain expectations.

We tend to **cooperate** with each other when we have conversations, generally sticking to the topic that is being discussed, or moving on to another topic in a way that allows others to understand. We

> **Key term**
>
> **Scheme:** a generally agreed or expected structure to a familiar type of interaction.

usually allow others to speak and have their turns, and we usually avoid speaking for too long. Most conversations stick to this scheme, but there are exceptions of course.

However, we also come across quite highly planned speech which clearly is not spontaneous and which is carefully designed to be effective to a particular audience.

Now look at the transcript that is presented below, which is taken from a speech by Michelle Obama to the Democratic Party convention in September 2012.

Like so many American families, our families weren't asking for much.

They didn't begrudge anyone else's success or care that others had much more than they did … in fact, they admired it.

They simply believed in that fundamental American promise that, even if you don't start out with much, if you work hard and do what you're supposed to do, then you should be able to build a decent life for yourself and an even better life for your kids and grandkids.

That's how they raised us … that's what we learned from their example.

We learned about dignity and decency – that how hard you work matters more than how much you make … that helping others means more than just getting ahead yourself.

We learned about honesty and integrity – that the truth matters … that you don't take shortcuts or play by your own set of rules … and success doesn't count unless you earn it fair and square.

We learned about gratitude and humility – that so many people had a hand in our success, from the teachers who inspired us to the janitors who kept our school clean … and we were taught to value everyone's contribution and treat everyone with respect.

Those are the values Barack and I – and so many of you – are trying to pass on to our own children.

That's who we are.

(Continues overleaf)

There is evidence of planning here because Michelle Obama establishes a focus (families) and then returns to it by using the pronoun 'they' to refer back. This creates cohesion: it helps the structure of the speech to hang together.

Here, Michelle Obama looks back again to summarise the points she made before and draw conclusions from the experiences. This time the pronoun 'that' helps to do this and gives cohesion to her speech. Again, this is clear evidence of planning.

The repetition of 'We learned about …' and 'that …' is an example of **rhetoric**. It has been planned to create a pattern to the speech, a pattern that helps emphasise the things Michelle Obama and her husband were taught to value.

Key term

Rhetoric: the art of using language persuasively and effectively.

The clever use of different pronouns here shows some planning. Obama uses I, you, our and we to show that what she has said is relevant to her personally, her as part of a couple, and to the audience in the hall and watching on TV too.

The way that Obama refers back to the time before her husband was president and then to the present day again shows some pre-planning. She wants to show that time has moved on and how that has made the president stronger, so she contrasts then and now.

This part of the speech uses clear signposting techniques, including 'You see ...' and 'And ...', all of which show some planning. She brings this part of the speech to a close by using 'But at the end of the day'. Looking back to the first part of the speech, she has gone from talking about family backgrounds and family values to focusing on how those values make the man whom she is describing. The whole speech has clearly been planned to pull these ideas together and present a coherent line for the audience to follow.

And standing before you four years ago, I knew that I didn't want any of that to change if Barack became president. Well, today, after so many struggles and triumphs and moments that have tested my husband in ways I never could have imagined, I have seen firsthand that being president doesn't change who you are – it reveals who you are.

You see, I've gotten to see up close and personal what being president really looks like.

And I've seen how the issues that come across a president's desk are always the hard ones – the problems where no amount of data or numbers will get you to the right answer ... the judgment calls where the stakes are so high, and there is no margin for error.

And as president, you can get all kinds of advice from all kinds of people.

But at the end of the day, when it comes time to make that decision, as president, all you have to guide you are your values, and your vision, and the life experiences that make you who you are.

Stretch yourself

Political speeches have always been a good resource for looking at how language can be planned very carefully to present a particular viewpoint, and there are some classics which people go back to time and time again.

Try to find some speeches from recent times that have not been studied much. Try to record a speech from one of the political parties' conferences, or an election speech at a school hustings or college council election. See if you can transcribe it and identify the features that show how planned it is.

Prepared speeches

As you have seen in the modelled example, planned speeches are often structured very carefully to show connections between ideas and to help develop a particular viewpoint. The modelled example above was a political speech, but we come across prepared speeches in all parts of our daily lives.

Activity 1

With a partner, brainstorm as many examples of planned speech as you can think of. Here are some places where you might hear them:

- school
- church
- work
- conference
- guided tour
- sporting event
- awards night.

Even planned speeches have to be spoken by a real person and to real audiences, and that means that good speakers will often use a script as a basis for what they say, rather than just recite it word for word. Many speakers **ad-lib** and turn the written, planned version into something more colloquial.

The extracts below are taken from the same speech by Bill Clinton in September 2012, but from two different sources. The speech was widely acclaimed – even by Clinton's political opponents – as being a very effective piece of **oratory**, because it sounded warm, genuine and down to earth.

The first extract is the script of his speech, as given to journalists before he delivered it. The second is a transcript of the actual speech, as he spoke it. Read the extracts and answer the questions that follow.

Key terms

Ad-lib: to make something up on the spot or to say something unprepared.
Oratory: public speaking; skill in public speaking.

Bill Clinton: script of speech

I understand the challenge we face. I know many Americans are still angry and frustrated with the economy. Though employment is growing, banks are beginning to lend and even housing prices are picking up a bit, too many people don't feel it.

I experienced the same thing in 1994 and early 1995. Our policies were working and the economy was growing but most people didn't feel it yet. By 1996, the economy was roaring, halfway through the longest peacetime expansion in American history.

President Obama started with a much weaker economy than I did. No president – not me or any of my predecessors could have repaired all the damage in just four years. But conditions are improving and if you'll renew the president's contract you will feel it.

I believe that with all my heart.

President Obama's approach embodies the values, the ideas, and the direction America must take to build a 21st century version of the American Dream in a nation of shared opportunities, shared prosperity and shared responsibilities.

Bill Clinton: transcript of actual speech

Now, look. Here's the challenge he faces and the challenge all of you who support him face. I get it. I know it. I've been there. A lot of Americans are still angry and frustrated about this economy. If you look at the numbers, you know employment is growing, banks are beginning to lend again. And in a lot of places, housing prices are even beginning to pick up.

But too many people do not feel it yet.

I had the same thing happen in 1994 and early '95. We could see that the policies were working, that the economy was growing. But most people didn't feel it yet. Thankfully, by 1996 the economy was roaring, everybody felt it, and we were halfway through the longest peacetime expansion in the history of the United States. But – (cheers, applause) – wait, wait. The difference this time is purely in the circumstances. President Obama started with a much weaker economy than I did. Listen to me, now. No president – no president, not me, not any of my predecessors, no one could have fully repaired all the damage that he found in just four years. (Cheers, applause.)

Now – but – (cheers, applause) – he has – he has laid the foundation for a new, modern, successful economy of shared prosperity. And if you will renew the president's contract, you will feel it. You will feel it. (Cheers, applause.)

Folks, whether the American people believe what I just said or not may be the whole election. I just want you to know that I believe it. With all my heart, I believe it. (Cheers, applause.)

Now, why do I believe it?

I'm fixing to tell you why. I believe it because President Obama's approach embodies the values, the ideas and the direction America has to take to build the 21st-century version of the American Dream: a nation of shared opportunities, shared responsibilities, shared prosperity, a shared sense of community.

Activity 2

a Note the parts of each text where you notice differences.

b Copy the table below and fill in five instances of the words and phrases Clinton has added in one column and the words and phrases he has changed in the other column.

Words and phrases added in actual speech	Words and phrases changed in actual speech
Now, look	
	Changes 'I experienced the same thing in 1994 and early 1995' to 'I had the same thing happen in 1994 and early 1995'

c Looking at the script, the transcript and your completed table above, what do you think are the main effects of what Clinton has done? Draw up a list of possible reasons with a partner. Here are some pointers to help you.

Activity 2 cont.

- How does the actual speech sound to you, compared with the script?
- Is it simpler?
- What does Clinton do more of in the spoken version?
- What does he simplify or change in the speech?

As you can see from Bill Clinton's speech, it is not just **what** you say that is important, but **how** you say it. He has made his carefully planned speech sound spontaneous in places and he has shown an awareness that his audience are actually there with him (even if millions of them are actually watching it on TV). But how easy is it to really do this? The following speaking and listening task asks you to try this out yourself.

Speaking and listening

Scripting to sound unscripted

Work in a small group of 3–4 students to do this speaking and listening task. You have been asked to prepare a speech to give in school about a plan to do one of the following (pick one):

- to introduce a school uniform
- to make all school dinners vegetarian-only
- to start the school day at 8am and end at 1pm
- to ban all mobile phones from school at all times.

Script a two-minute speech on your chosen topic and then try it out on other people in your group. Then try to redraft it, thinking of areas where you could build in more casual, colloquial language and ad-libs that make you come across as more relaxed and genuine than the scripted version. How effective are your changes? How easy is it to script something to sound like it is unscripted?

It is not just set-piece political speeches that require planning, but other types of talk too. Try the following task, which asks you to rank different types of talk in order of how planned or unplanned they might be.

Activity 3

Have a look at the list below of different types of talk. In pairs, can you diamond rank them in order of how planned or unplanned you think they might be and give reasons for your choices? Put the ones you think are most planned at the top of the diamond and those that are most spontaneous at the bottom.

i   A sermon by a priest in a church

ii   Answering a phone call from a friend

iii   Answering a phone call from a number you do not recognise

iv   A teacher starting a lesson that is being observed by an Ofsted inspector

v   A street charity collector trying to get you to sign up to their cause

vi   Three friends playing Xbox live together over the internet

vii   A parent asking you about your day at school

viii Buying a book of stamps from a shop assistant

ix   A radio presenter commentating on a Paralympics event

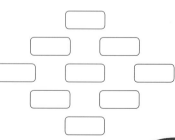

One way of testing out the differences between planned and unplanned speech is to carry out a simple experiment. Get hold of a digital voice recorder or mobile phone with a voice recording facility and then set up the following:

- Think of a location in your school or college.
- Ask one friend to give directions to that location and record them as they speak.
- Then tell another friend that they have two minutes to prepare their directions.
- Give them two minutes to plan, and then record them giving you the directions.
- Transcribe and compare the different recordings.
- What do you notice about the differences between the spontaneous and planned versions?
- Remember: get permission from all of those you are recording!

Spontaneous and semi-planned speech

Unplanned speech is one of the most common types of speech that we use. It often consists of a number of features that you will see in other units, such as non-fluency features (pauses and fillers), self-corrections (where the speaker rephrases in a more effective way something they have started to say), interruptions and overlaps from other speakers (where other speakers stop you from talking by speaking themselves, or say things to support what you are saying), and is often lacking in the kind of signposting that we find in planned, prepared speech.

However, that does not necessarily make it less clear or less effective. If you think about most conversations that you have, they generally do the job quite well. In fact, spontaneous speech is often really well suited to dealing with how things change in a conversation and for being flexible. It is also very useful when describing events that are changing around us.

The transcript below is taken from two friends playing a game together on Xbox Live. They are in different parts of the country but are playing on the same game and working together on the same team.

Top tip

Be careful not to describe spoken language as 'incorrect' or 'wrong'. When you are studying language, it is best to talk about spoken language as 'non-standard' if it does not follow the usual patterns of written language.

L: over there (1) yeah (.) wait (.) **wait**

F: where are they

L: can't see them yet (.) //just//

F: //there look he's coming over (.) he's crossing the bridge=

L: =get him (.) **Get** him quick (.)

F: I need more ammo

L: you've just got to hit him

F: got to get to cover

L: wait (.) cover me (.) he's in the barn (.) you come to me (.) yeah

F: right (.) can't see him (.) where are you

L: by the wall (.) next (.) next to the oil drums (.) you get here and we'll (1) stop (.) wait (.) he's there in the (.) the window

F: who got him

L: what

F: someone got him

L: not me

F: uh-oh

Activity 1

a Pick out five moments from this transcript which indicate that it has not been planned.

b What reasons can you come up with for why the speech is so spontaneous?

c If the boys were playing the game together in the same room, do you think the transcript might be any different?

One thing you have probably noticed from the transcript above is that a great deal of spontaneous speech relies on events that are happening around us at a given time and are very much **context dependent**. This means that speakers have to think on their feet and respond to what is happening, rather than planning out what they are saying. This leads to quite short utterances and a large amount of cooperation between the two players. For example, when they are trying to work out who has shot their enemy they work this out together.

Key terms

Context dependent: relying on the immediate environment to make complete sense.

Turn-taking: the normal structure of conversations in which one speaker's turn (what they have to say) is followed by another's.

F: who got him

L: what

F: someone got him

L: not me

F: uh-oh

Another form of spontaneous speech that we frequently hear around us is the live commentary. In a commentary, the speaker has to describe what is happening at that moment. When this is for TV, the viewers can see the action being described – football match, Paralympic event, demonstration against government cuts – so the commentary offers an interpretation and often a narrative (or storyline) for viewers to follow. However, when commentaries are for a radio audience, there is more to describe so that the audience can visualise events.

The following extract is taken from a commentary that accompanied a stage of the Tour of Britain cycle race on TV. Read the extract and see if you can answer the questions that follow it.

C1: stage 5 of the Tour of Britain will take the riders from Trentham Gardens through to Hanley in Stoke-on-Trent (.) a distance of 147 kilometres (.) and one of the toughest stages (.) they've always proved to be (.) real characters in the history of this race (1) Bradley Wiggins (.) well just rolling away at the front there with Mark Cavendish (.) in the IG Markets gold jersey (1) ahead of them (.) well (.) a tough test (.) will Cavendish be able to keep the lead

C2: an extremely difficult stage we've got here in Stoke (.) Bradley Wiggins there (.) riding alongside his team leader Mark Cavendish in that IG gold jersey

C1: the flags are out (.) in support in support of Mark Cavendish there's Christian Howes leader in the King of the mountains and riding alongside him Pete Williams (.) leader in the Yodel Sprint competition (3) well here's a shot of the tail of the peloton (.) already the speed is **very** high as you can see **oh there's a crash** (.) now who's gone **ooh** several riders have hit the deck (.) and that's one of the members of the Liquigas team (.) that's Borgini=

C2:   =yeah Borgini from Liquigas down (.) and Brett Lancaster there (.) also on the floor (.) facing backwards actually (1) several riders (.) gone down (1) Borgini looks in all sorts of trouble (1)

Activity 2

a   How can you tell that the commentators are describing something as it happens? Ring examples of where you think this is clear.

b   What tense is being used in most of the verbs here? See if you can pick out examples.

c   Can you identify the different roles of the two commentators? How do they work together to describe events as they happen?

Stretch yourself

As well as TV and radio commentaries, a fairly new form has emerged online. This is the text commentary, which provides regularly updated written commentary on games. Again, like other CMC forms that you have already looked at – text messaging, social networking, online chat – these are not strictly spoken language, but show many of the same features of spontaneous talk.

Have a look at this extract from a football text commentary and see if you can work out what makes it similar to and different from the spoken commentary you have looked at above.

13 mins GOAL
Bayern Munich 0–1 Real Madrid

In the first game of the group stage, you don't want to give a goal away like this! Angel di Maria curls over a wickedly inswinging corner from the right and Pepe gets the flick-on. Neuer comes out to punch, misses and Benzema is left with a simple tap-in. First blood to the Spanish champions.

18 mins

What a start from Real, they are really playing a clever attacking game. An excellent first-time pass by Alonso almost puts Ronaldo clear down the left, but for the last ditch interception by Philip Lahm.

SOMEONE LIVE *Radio's Alvin Hunsen*

Xabi Alonso and Mesut Ozil seem to have free rein of the midfield and Real look dangerous on the flanks. It feels like it will only be a matter of time before Ronaldo will show his class. It's just great that they've come to give it a good go!

25 mins CHANCE!

Against the run of play di Maria dawdles on the ball and Schweinsteiger dispossesses him and Bayern are counterattacking. Martinez moves the ball forward quickly into the box, but Mario Gomez's snapshot lack the precision to beat Casillas, who makes a good sharp save.

SOMEONE LIVE *Radio's Matt Twiddle*

At the moment it looks like Bayern are slowly coming back into the game – Schweinsteiger's influence is growing.

30 mins RED CARD & PENALTY TO REAL!
Ronaldo once again receives the ball in space, on the right this time and he's away and into the box he beats Badstuber for pace and knocks the ball past Neuer, who clips the Portuguese's cleverly trailing foot. That's a penalty and referee Olsen reaches for his top pocket. Bayern are really up against it now! An hour with ten men and probably 2-0 down.

Other conversations that occur in everyday speech might have a degree of planning involved. For example, when one speaker is having a conversation that is linked to their job, they may well use a similar structure each time they encounter the same situation. While the speakers are not really working to a script, they are so used to situations like this that they follow a formula.

One such situation in which there is often a mixture of planned and unplanned speech is the classroom. Many different types of talk happen in classrooms, ranging from prepared speeches to completely spontaneous conversations. Often, the teacher has planned a structure to the lesson but this does not mean that he or she will necessarily have prepared the exact words to use. Then again, there are some situations where teachers may well say nearly the same thing in every lesson, or take part in exchanges with different classes and students that follow almost identical patterns.

The transcript below is taken from a lesson in which the teacher (A) is introducing some guests to the class. The students are the other speakers.

A: can I introduce some people here (.) who've given up their time and their considerable expertise (.) they work for Saatchi's which is one of the biggest advertising agencies in the world OK (.) they have already (.) been working on your ideas (1) [shows poster to class]

F: [reading from poster of Wayne Rooney] earns 10 times more than a school teacher

B: I like //that//

D: //yeah//

A: Do you like this one= [showing poster of David Beckham]

C: =I love David Beckham

A: yeah

C: what's that say

A: [reading from poster] no I got the snakeskin interior with teak //design//

C: //no that's mean// I like David Beckham

F: [laughter]

A: ok (.) Henry

D: yeah

A: do you remember the other day when you made a speech

D: yeah

A: right what did you make a speech about

D: cannabis

A: cannabis (.) and what did you say about cannabis

D: how it should be legalized=

A: =and what was one of the points that //Danielle// made can you remember

E: //tax// tax

A: correct (.) what do you think of that then [holds up poster]

F: [reading from poster] let's make cash from hash [laughter]

A: any idea you take you can turn into an advert right (.) Now listen (.) Nana-Kwame and Michael (.) you told me (.) you were gonna work (.) on a campaign about knife crime and youth //services// right

G: //yes//

A: this chap over here (.) //right//

G: //the good looking fella//

A: this is Chris right (1) Chris (.) is a designer and he's gonna start to design stuff as we discuss it (.) so Nana-Kwame you start to tell us about your (.) idea you and Michael right (1) what is your point you start telling us your point (.) about knife crime and youth services (.) and this guy will do you an advert

Activity 3

a Who do you think sounds most prepared in this transcript? Point to examples to illustrate your view.

b How does the teacher use language to keep the students involved in what is going on? Again point to examples.

c One planned structure that is very common in classroom exchanges is the three-part exchange, where the teacher asks a question, a student responds and the teacher then comments on the response. Can you see any examples of this structure in the transcript? Why might this be an effective structure to use in a lesson?

Represented speech

As well as real spoken language, you will also come across written language that is designed to look or sound like speech. Writers of soap operas and dramas and authors of fiction often try to make the speech of their characters sound like genuine speech. But there can be problems with this, because as you can see from the extract below which is from a transcript of five family members in the same room, not all spoken language is necessarily that easy to follow.

A: any idea where the remote for the TV is

B: is that your cup on the floor

C: err (.) yeah

B: why is it lying there

C: I was going to take it back in a minute

D: you always leave your stuff lying around

C: shut up

B: can you help Daddy find the remote please

C: the what

Activity 1

a Why might this be difficult to follow?

b If you were scripting a family conversation, what would you take out to make this easier to follow?

c What would you add to make this easier to follow?

The following is an extract from the novel *Pigeon English* by Stephen Kelman. The narrator, Harrison, is watching his older sister have her hair done with some of her friends. Read the extract and then do the activities that follow.

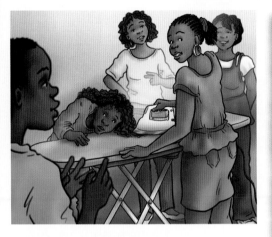

Miquita was ironing Lydia's hair. Mamma go sound her when she finds out.

Me: I bet it goes on fire.

Lydia: How! No, it won't.

Me: I bet it does.

Lydia: Don't disturb!

Me: I can watch if I want. Lydia can't stop me watching. I'm the man of the house.

Lydia: Just don't burn me, OK?

Miquita: Don't worry, man. I've done it enough times.

Chanelle: Twice.

Miquita: So? I'm well skilful, innit. My auntie taught me, she learnt it in the pen.

Activity 2

a In what ways do you think the author has managed to make this sound like unplanned, spontaneous speech? Pick out examples from the text.

b Why do you think the author has used this style? Does it add anything to the story?

c What other features that the writer has used make this sound like genuine speech?

The following transcript is taken from a scripted TV show called *Friday Night Dinner*. As it is scripted, it is designed to be spoken, but it does not contain all the features of spontaneous talk. The boys, Adam and Johnny, have just come home to find a neighbour using the toilet. They go into the garage to see their parents (M and D).

M: hi boys

J: what you doing in the garage

M: we're having a clear out

A: don't you mean 'what's Jim doing in our loo'

M: Martin you do know the boys are here (.) say hello

D: what d (.) oh hello bambinos

J: no top tonight

M: he's boiling=

D: =I'm boiling

A: and Jim's using our toilet because=

M: =oh his is broken=

J: =broken

M: he broke it [points to box] no there

A: he broke his own toilet (.) how did he do that

M: how do I know anyway (.) he asked if he could use ours (.) what could I say

A: no

J: use a bucket

D: [points to a pile of magazines] them as well

M: **yes** (.) all of them and you're doing the sofa bed

D: your mother wants me to chuck away all my copies of New Scientist magazine (.) can you believe it

A: yes

M: thank you Adam

D: what do you mean 'yes'

M: you don't even **read** them why do you keep all this crap

D: it's not **crap** (.) I wish you'd stop calling it crap (.) they're collectables

A: are they

D: boys look (.) this one (.) is from 1969 and (.) there's a (.) poster of Isaac Newton (.) now he was a gen//ius//

M: //sorry// I'm not discussing Isaac Newton again (1) tomorrow morning you are taking them all to the dump (.) **impossible**

D: Newton

A: crap

J: crap

Activity 3

a In what ways do you think that this extract uses elements of genuinely spontaneous speech?

b In what ways do you think it is **not** like genuinely spontaneous speech?

c Now, try to work out how you would turn an extract of genuine speech into a script. Which parts would you leave out and which parts would you include? What factors might influence you in making these decisions?

Check your learning

In this unit you have covered quite a lot of different ideas. Think about the following terms and see if you can write your own definition for each of them.

- Spontaneous speech
- Rhetorical technique
- Ad-lib
- Colloquial
- Scheme
- Context-dependent speech

For each of the terms above, try to think of different types of talk in which they might occur. Which ones might appear in each of the following? You might find that some of these use two or more features.

- A political speech
- A sermon by a priest
- A chat between friends
- An apology you have to make when you have been caught doing something you should not have been doing
- A conversation with a shop assistant when you are buying something
- A weather forecast on the TV
- A newsreader's introduction to a programme
- An online chat with a group of friends
- A speech at a school council meeting
- A TV chef explaining a recipe

6

Implied meanings: Why don't you say what you mean?

As you have seen, conversations generally work because the people involved in the conversation stick to a set of unwritten rules. We know when we are supposed to talk, we understand that certain questions or statements require certain responses and we adapt the way that we speak and the words we choose to use to suit the circumstances. However, we do not always say what we mean and the signals become confused.

For example, you might ask a friend if they want to see a film and they might reply that they have already seen it. The answer implies that they do not want to see the film again, but they have not **explicitly** said this; maybe they do want to see it again because they loved it so much. When we do not say what we mean, we imply meaning and this can lead to misunderstandings.

Also, people sometimes imply meanings on purpose; they might be trying to avoid an argument or they may be afraid of being too direct. Imagine if a friend's mum asked you if you liked the cake that she made, and you did not. Most people would find a way of implying what they think rather than being brutally honest and just saying, 'No it's disgusting'!

The script below is from the comedy series *The Inbetweeners*. A student, Will, is starting a new school and is in a meeting for new students with the head of Sixth Form, Mr Gilbert. The comments on the following transcript should help you to recognise how identifying and explaining implied meanings can help you to write about spoken language.

Key term

Explicit meaning: the meaning is very clear and there is no room for interpretation. The opposite of implied meaning.

Will is implying that Mr Gilbert will agree with him. By flattering him first, he avoids confrontation.

Mr Gilbert's sarcastic response picks up on the implications of the word 'seem'; for Will the word was an attempt to establish an equal footing, for Mr Gilbert it is a veiled insult.

Obviously, as a senior teacher, Mr Gilbert is not insecure about learning, and he is not pleased to be spoken to about his intelligence. Here Mr Gilbert uses polite words such as lovely and nice but they actually imply disapproval.

Will: Mr Gilbert (.) you seem like an intelligent man

Mr Gilbert: Ah (.) I seem intelligent. How lovely of you to say

Will: No no I just meant

Mr Gilbert: Well I've long been insecure about my capacity for learning so it's nice to have it ratified by you (.) a child

Will: What I meant was (.) do you think that these badges which single us out as new kids are a good idea

> Will asks a direct question, so the form of the sentence is a question. However, if you look at what Will actually intends to say, you could say that the sentence's function is that of a statement. Something like, 'These badges are a stupid idea.'

Mr Gilbert: Yes (.) and if you have any more views on it I suggest you join the school debating society (.) obviously you'll have to start one first

> Mr Gilbert answers Will's question explicitly, showing Will that at this school, teachers are not willing to enter into discussion with students about their decisions.

Speaking and listening

Working in a pair, imagine that one of you is a head teacher and one is a new student. The student is trying to persuade the head teacher that he need not attend an assembly where new students have to stand up and introduce themselves.

Unlike Mr Gilbert, you are a head teacher who is a bit more welcoming. However, you do not like having your ideas challenged. Role play how both parties attempt to get their own way.

'That is not what I meant': implied meanings and misunderstandings

A very common example of how implied meaning can cause misunderstandings is when you talk to young children. As children learn to talk they have a huge number of rules to take on board. They have got to figure out all of the words they need, how to pronounce them and how to put them in the right order. It is not surprising that when adults speak to children, they do not always get the answers that they expect. Look at the two snippets of conversation below.

(Phone call)

Adult: hi. Is mummy there?

Child: yes (puts phone down)

(At a party)

Child: can I have some more Coke?

Mum: don't you think you've had enough?

Child: no

> So, you can see that when adults imply meaning, children can often take them at face value and misunderstandings occur.

Speaking and listening

a   Work with a partner. Look at the two snippets of speech above. For each one, discuss what you think the child thought the adult meant, rather than the adult's implied meaning.   *(Continues overleaf)*

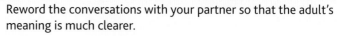

b   Reword the conversations with your partner so that the adult's meaning is much clearer.

c   Look at the following statements. Can you explain how they might be misunderstood by a child?

    i   (At dinner time) Are you hungry?

    ii   (At the park) I'm tired now.

    iii   Look at this mess.

    iv   I can't believe you're not tired yet.

    v   How many times have I told you to not run off?

However, even in adult conversations, a statement is not always as obvious as it looks. Unless we explicitly say what we want, we are open to being misunderstood. Look at these two snippets of conversation and answer the questions below.

1

Woman: I'm freezing

Man: Put your coat on

2

Woman: I haven't got change for the bus

Man: Oh dear

Activity 1

a   What other responses could have been offered in reply to the two statements above? Write down an alternative to each answer from the man.

b   What do you think the woman actually meant in each case? What could she have said in order to be clearer?

c   Copy the table below and fill it in with your own examples of phrases that could have more than one meaning? Try to think of two more examples yourself.

A phrase which could have more than one meaning	One meaning	An alternative meaning
'I'm starving'	'Let's stop for food'	'Give me some of your food'
'It's cold in here'		
'Don't look at me like that'		
'Something smells tasty'		

'Do not talk to me like that': politeness and context

Another reason that meanings can be implied is that it would seem rude in some circumstances to request things directly. Whereas some implied meanings are just open to being misunderstood, sometimes we use them in order to deliberately cloud the issue. If you think of your own day-to-day interaction, you automatically switch the style of language to suit the person that you are talking to. This applies to meanings as well as more obvious things such as lexis or your accent.

In the following activity, you can look at the many different ways that you could ask for the same thing. In this case, imagine that you want to use the phone. Here are some of the ways that you could ask for the phone.

- Give me the phone!
- When are you going to be finished?
- Can I have the phone after you please?
- Hurry up!
- I'll need the phone in a minute!
- Are you going to be all day?
- Phone!

'Give me the phone' is the most direct; there is no confusion about what the speaker wants. It is also quite rude and may have the opposite effect on the person you are speaking to.

Speaking and listening

a Work in a group of four. Look at the list and put the statements in order from the most **direct** to the most indirect.

b Use a similar request, this time to borrow a pen, and describe how you would alter the phrases depending on your audience.

To your grandma	*Granny, do you have a pen I can use?*
To a teacher	
To your mum	
To a shopkeeper	
To a friend	
To your sister/brother	
To a stranger	

c Which of your examples is the rudest? Is it also the most direct? Does this mean that implied meanings are generally a more polite way to use language?

The transcript on page 76 is from the reality TV programme
Educating Essex. In the dialogue below, the teacher Mr Drew is in conversation with a pupil called Charlotte who has been in a lot of trouble recently. Mr Drew is trying to tell Charlotte off but her friends are making her laugh. Following on from our earlier discussion about how sometimes people deliberately imply meanings, we are going to look at how both participants refuse to move from their position and what their words actually imply.

> **Key term**
>
> **Direct:** to be explicit in putting forward your thoughts.

Mr Drew uses formal language that reinforces his position of authority.

The fact that Charlotte is laughing suggests that she is not taking Mr Drew's authority seriously. It may be that they have a quite friendly relationship. It could also be because Charlotte's friends are watching her and she is showing them that she does not respect Mr Drew.

Although Charlotte has been asked a direct question, she does not answer it directly. It could be because she does not want to lose face in front of her friends. It could also be an attempt to tell Mr Drew that she is not laughing at him but at her friends. Either way, it is not the response that Mr Drew expects.

By repeating the question, Mr Drew is indicating to Charlotte that he wants her to respect his authority by answering his question directly. The content of the question is irrelevant; now the conversation is about control.

Mr D: I do not wish to experience your unpleasantness so do not make me experience it

C: (laughing) all right

Mr D: am I amused

C: (pointing at a friend) he's laughing at me

Mr D: am I amused

C: don't know are you

Mr D: am I amused

C: don't know are you

Mr D: do you think I'm amused

C: don't know (.) maybe

Mr D: OK we're doing this until you give the correct answer

C: (laughs)

Mr D: will I be amused

C: I don't know cos I'm not you

Mr D: do you think I'll be amused (.) have a guess Charlotte (.) do you think I'll be amused

C: one day maybe I don't know

Mr D: do you think I will be amused

C: oh my God

Mr D: do you think I'll be amused

C: (laughing) I can't stop laughing

Activity 1

a Mr Drew repeats the word 'amused' over and over again. Suggest why he has heavily emphasised on this particular word? What does 'amuse' imply in this conversation?

b i Why does Charlotte not answer Mr D directly? What limitations are there in her language choices?

  ii What does the phrase 'Oh my God' imply here?

c Think of other contexts where the relationship between people affects how direct they can be. List five examples of your own. For example, a mobile phone salesman:

Customer: what phone is the best

Salesman: well it depends how much money you want to spend (implies: well obviously the most expensive ones are the best)

So far, the evidence in this unit does suggest that the more polite we intend to be, the more we rely on implied meanings in order to achieve this. However, the following transcript illustrates that politeness can sometimes be quite threatening. The transcript below is from Channel 4's evening news programme and is a discussion about the Government's U-turn on fuel tax.

Krishnan: well earlier I spoke to the Economic Secretary to the Treasury Chloë Smith and I asked her why the Government is spending money that it doesn't have

Chloë: well this is money that will be accounted for of course this is money that is er going to come from departmental underspend and we'll be coming back with more details of that at the Autumn statement

Krishnan: so at the moment it is an unfunded tax cut

Chloë: no this is money that we are gaining from er department underspends as I //said//

Krishnan: //where//

Chloë: we– we as I say from departmental underspend from departments which have underspent and we have a number of those and we'll be able to come back at Autumn statement to give full details //of those//

Krishnan: //so you// don't know at the moment

Chloë: the work is of course progressing to ensure that er it is possible to give you er a full range at the Autumn statement

Krishnan: is it possible that there isn't a half a billion pounds worth

Chloë: we we we are confident we have the er funds available er to make this policy work and the point //is//

Krishnan: //confident// but not certain

Chloë: this is a funded policy the point is (.) the real //point is//

Krishnan: //but// it is not funded because you can't tell me how it is funded

Chloë: the //the//

Krishnan: //you're// thinking it will be

Chloë: I'll be able to give you detail at the Autumn statement

Newsreaders such as Krishnan Guru-Murthy may rely on implied meaning to get their point across

> **Top tip**
>
> Political interviews offer a lot of ground for exploring implied meanings, especially when politicians want to avoid being pinned down to committing to a policy which has not been fully discussed. Watch programmes such as *Question Time* or *Newsnight* and see if you can identify examples of implied meaning.

a Look at Krishnan's turns. Rather like Mr Drew in the previous transcript, he repeats himself a lot. He might not say the same words like Mr Drew's 'Am I amused?' but he does repeat a certain idea. Can you identify what idea he is repeating and what the implied criticism is?

b Although Chloë Smith talks quite a lot, she does not say very much. What phrases does she keep repeating? Is there an implied meaning at play here too?

c As you have seen in Unit 2 on interactions, interruptions can be rude but they can also be cooperative. What purpose do you think Krishnan's interruptions have here?

Top tip

In your answers, give an example of a context as well as how implied meaning could be used. Use the example above as a guide.

Stretch yourself

Work with a partner. Take the same structure as this transcript. Use a current news story and role play how the presenter tries to force the interviewee into a corner. Think about how many of the things that you say are explicit and how many are implied. Is there an equal balance between the two participants?

Using implied meaning to persuade

Sometimes people have conversations where they have a clear outcome in mind but they know that the negotiations might be difficult. There are lots of everyday examples of this, ranging from the trivial or trying to get your parents to give you a lift, to the more important such as being allowed to go somewhere that your family does not approve of. This is where it can be said that there is a **subtext** to the conversation.

In the transcript below, you can see examples of subtext and implied meanings. Tom clearly wants to persuade his mother about something but he knows that she will not agree with him.

Read this transcript from the Channel 4 documentary *The Family*. Tom and his mum are alone and Tom instigates this conversation about his school.

Key term

Subtext: similar to an implied meaning and describes the concept that what we say is not necessarily what we mean.

T: mum can I talk to you about the school thing

M: no (.) you have to talk to dad

T: I want to talk to //you//

M: //no// because I get into trouble

T: I want to talk to you first (.) we'll say that we haven't talked //but//

M: //no// because it always comes out and I get into trouble (2)

T: no (.) well (4)

M: could I be right in thinking you just don't like any school you've been to

T: no but I don't like school

M: oh //well//

T: //they// push you too //hard//

M: //well// because you're a bright boy

T: but they push you too hard

M: but they only expect what they know you can achieve

T: no they don't

M: yeah they do it's just you need to put in a bit of effort

T: I do put in effort

M: when do you put in effort (.) I've never seen you doing any homework

T: that's cos I don't have em

M: that's cos you don't do it

T: I don't wanna be at that school mum I hate it

M: what what

T: I hate it they shout at you for a small thing cos our school is so strict an' all this pressure to do well

M: it's good

Activity 1

a
i What is Tom trying to achieve in this conversation?
ii What words does Tom use to make his mum feel sorry for him?
iii Do you think that Tom is successful? What is your evidence for this?

b
i What is Tom's mum trying to achieve?
ii How does Tom's mum's tone change in the conversation?

c
Make two lists: words that Mum uses to encourage Tom and words used to assert her authority.

Remind yourself of the misunderstandings that we saw at the beginning of this unit. We discussed how one phrase, for example 'I'm starving', could actually have another meaning, such as 'Get me some food'.

Apply this to the smaller section of the conversation between Tom and his mum below. We are going to focus on when the sentences used by Tom or his mum look like statements but are actually disguised commands.

When Tom says, 'But they push you too hard', although this is a statement it could also be understood as a **command**, something like, 'take me out of that school'. This is another way of implying meaning.

Key term

Command: an utterance where one speaker tells another to carry out an action.

Text A

Tom has a clear agenda in this conversation and he knows that his mum is the better parent to discuss this with. Nonetheless he still has to convince her that he is unhappy at the school and is not just trying to avoid hard work. He tries to achieve this by implying that the teachers are cruel and that he is victimised, using words like 'pressure' and 'push'. He avoids directly asking to leave the school until the very end of the conversation, using statements like 'they push you too hard' in order to make his mum feel sorry for him.

T: //they push you too hard

M: well because you're a bright boy

T: but they push you too hard

M: but they only expect what they know you can achieve

T: no they don't

M: yeah they do it's just you need to put in a bit of effort

T: I do put in effort

M: when do you put in effort (.) I've never seen you doing any homework

T: that's cos I don't have em

M: that's cos you don't do it

Another example of when a sentence's form is different to its actual function is when Mum says 'When do you put in effort?'. You could say that Mum's question is implying some criticism rather than asking a question to which she wants a reply. What might that statement be?

By looking at the implied meanings and the choice of sentences used by Tom and his mum, you can start to develop an analysis of their conversation that goes beyond describing what they feel and think and explores how they use spoken language to express themselves. In an essay, you might write about the conversation as in Text A, with a focus on the implied meaning rather than the actual words.

Activity 2

Write a similar paragraph in which you focus on what Mum wants to achieve in the conversation.

Speaking and listening

In a pair, role play some of the following scenarios making a conscious effort to use sentences that avoid being direct.

Scenario 1

A: You are a customer returning a faulty item of clothing. You have actually worn it but the zip broke immediately so you are determined to get your money back.

B: You are the shop assistant and you can see that the item has been worn. You are reluctant to refund the customer but must stay polite throughout the conversation.

Scenario 2

A: You are a door-to-door salesperson trying to sell overpriced kitchen equipment. You are very persistent and do not take no for an answer.

B: You are the householder and you do not want to buy anything but you do not want to be rude.

Scenario 3

A: You are a taxi driver moaning about cyclists and how they have no road sense.

B: You are the passenger, a keen cyclist. You do not want to get into an argument but at the same time you cannot really agree with the taxi driver.

Arguments and quarrels

So far we have looked at:

- how implied meanings can sometimes be misunderstood
- the ways in which implied meanings can help us to be polite
- how the context in which we are talking affects the extent to which we use implied meanings
- how we use implied meanings to try to get our own way.

It is harder for someone to turn you down if you have not explicitly asked for something. Lastly we are going to look at the times when implied meanings signal arguments or problematic relationships. These are particularly useful to look at when analysing scripted language.

In the play *Death of a Salesman* by Arthur Miller, the relationships between different members of a family give rise to arguments and uneasiness. In the following scene, early on in the play, two brothers, Biff and Happy, are discussing their father's strange behaviour. Biff has recently returned from travelling in Texas.

Biff: Why does Dad mock me all the time?

Happy: He's not mocking you, he-

Biff: Everything I say there's a twist of mockery on his face. I can't get near him.

Happy: He just wants you to make good, that's all. I wanted to talk to you about Dad for a long time, Biff. Something's – happening to him. He – talks to himself.

Biff: I noticed that this morning. But he always mumbled.

Happy: But not so noticeable. It got so embarrassing I sent him to Florida. And you know something? Most of the time he's talking to you.

Biff: What's he say about me?

Happy: I can't make it out.

Biff: What's he say about me?

Happy: I think the fact that you're not settled, that you're still kind of up in the air . . .

Biff: There's one or two other things depressing him, Happy.

Happy: What do you mean?

Biff: Never mind. Just don't lay it all to me.

Happy: But I think if you got started – I mean – is there any future for you out there?

Activity 1

a Choosing from the list of adjectives below, describe the relationship between the two brothers in this scene? When you have chosen the adjectives, give reasons for your choices.

- Intimate
- Caring
- Unfriendly
- Hostile
- Cautious
- Distrustful

b The whole dialogue appears to be about avoiding speaking directly. Copy the table below and fill it in with what you think the brothers really mean, or are implying.

Line from the play	What it really means
Example: *He's not mocking you, he –*	*He's not mocking you he is just disappointed in you.*
'He just wants you to make good'	
'Something's happening to him'	
'That you're still kind of up in the air'	
'There's one or two other things depressing him, Happy'	
'Just don't lay it all to me'	
'But I think if you got started'	

c Look back at the work that you did in the unit on non-fluency. Happy uses a lot of non-fluency features in this scene. Identify them and suggest why he uses them here.

In another scene in the same play, Biff and Happy are talking to their mother, Linda.

Activity 2

a What would you say the topic of this conversation is? Is it the same as its purpose?

b Is there an implied meaning when Biff says, 'I don't want my old pal looking old'? What do you think the underlying message might be?

c Happy says 'He admires Pop'. What do you think the word 'admires' implies? How is this different to how Linda wants Biff to feel about his Pop?

Biff: Your hair ... (He touches her hair) Your hair got so grey.

Linda: Oh, it's been grey since you were in high school. I just stopped dyeing it, that's all.

Biff: Dye it again will ya? I don't want my old pal looking old. (He smiles)

Linda: You're such a boy! You think you can go away for a year and ... You've got to get it into your head now that one day you'll knock on this door and there'll be strange people here –

Biff: What are you talking about? You're not even sixty, Mom.

Linda: But what about your father?

Biff: (lamely) Well, I meant him too.

Happy: He admires Pop.

Linda: Biff, dear, if you don't have any feeling for him, then you can't have any for me.

Biff: Sure I can Mom.

In a later scene from *Death of a Salesman*, Willy, the father of Happy and Biff, has gone to his boss and attempted to ask for more money and a less stressful job. He ends up getting sacked.

Howard: Willy, look …

Willy: I'll go to Boston.

Howard: Willy, you can't go to Boston for us.

Willy: Why can't I go?

Howard: I don't want you to represent us. I've been meaning to tell you for a long time now.

Willy: Howard, are you firing me?

Howard: I think you need a good long rest, Willy.

Willy: Howard –

Howard: And when you feel better, come back and we'll see if we can work something out.

Willy: But I gotta earn money, Howard. I'm in no position to –

Howard: Where are your sons? Why don't your sons give you a hand?

Willy: They're working on a very big deal.

Howard: This is no time for false pride, Willy. You go to your sons and you tell them that you're tired. You've got two great boys, haven't you?

Willy: Oh, no question, no question, but in the meantime …

Howard: Then that's that, heh?

Willy: Allright, I'll go to Boston tomorrow.

Howard: No, no.

Willy: I can't throw myself on my sons. I'm not a cripple!

Howard: Look, kid, I'm busy this morning.

Willy: Howard, you've got to let me go to Boston!

Howard: (*hard, keeping himself under control*) I've got a line of people to see this morning. Sit down, take five minutes, and pull yourself together, and then go home, will ya? I need the office Willy.

Activity 3

a Thinking back on the work that we have done on implication, apply this to Howard's language. How many times in the script does Howard say that he is firing Willy?

b Look at the statements below with a partner and think about whether you agree or disagree with the following statements. For each one, write down if you agree or disagree and give an example from the script to back up your answer.

Statement	Agree/disagree	Explanation and evidence
Willy is desperate to keep his job.	*Agree*	*I agree because Willy wilfully misunderstands Howard's attempt to sack him.*
Willy does not think his sons can help him financially.		
Howard is kind to Willy.		
Willy is bad at his job.		
Howard patronises Willy.		
Willy is optimistic about the future.		

C   It must difficult to sack someone, especially if they beg for their job. Write a script where someone is being sacked. Your aim is to make the audience feel supportive of the employee and to dislike the boss.

Speaking and listening

Role play a situation where one person is a boss and the other person is an employee about to be sacked. To make this task challenging, the boss must avoid actually saying the words 'you're sacked' or 'you're fired'; all of the meaning in their speech is implied. On the other hand, the employee must be like Willy, someone who refuses to understand that he is being sacked. You can choose the type of job that is being discussed, but try to stick closely to the suggested speech styles.

Check your learning

Explain four different ways in which you can explore implied meanings in conversation.

Describe some different contexts or scenarios that are more likely to involve implied meanings and some that are not.

You have also looked at the way the form of some sentences is different to their actual function. Describe how this works, giving an example from one of the transcripts in the unit.

7

Attitudes to spoken language: 'It ain't what you say, it's the way that you say it'

This book has introduced you to the way in which spoken language is used in a different way to written English. You will have explored the ways:

- in which people use spoken language according to the context
- to describe the patterns and features of language that are used in speech.

Most importantly, you should know how you can use spoken language yourself to get your message across in the best way.

This unit explores the way spoken language can cause certain reactions in people. The way in which actors choose to speak is often related to the way that they want to present their characters' personality. For example, the actor David Tennant has a Scottish accent and yet the accent that he used for Doctor Who was southern English. Why was this? Why should an accent make a difference if the words are the same? Does the way in which you talk actually matter?

To answer these questions we are going to pull together what we already know about spoken language and look at some writers' attitudes towards spoken language. We are going to look at a range of articles; things that people have written that show their strong feelings about the way that people use spoken English.

Actors such as Scot David Tennant often use different accents for different roles.

Speaking and listening

Before we look at other people's viewpoints, let us think about yours. Do you ever judge people because of the way they use language? Discuss this in pairs, look at the mind-map and add any other ideas of your own.

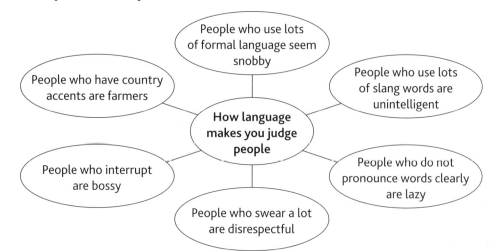

- People who use lots of formal language seem snobby
- People who have country accents are farmers
- People who use lots of slang words are unintelligent
- How language makes you judge people
- People who interrupt are bossy
- People who do not pronounce words clearly are lazy
- People who swear a lot are disrespectful

Do you agree with any of the ideas above? Some of them could be deemed to be prejudiced. Why do you think this may be the case?

Accents

What is an accent? Lots of people think that they do not have an accent, that only those different from them have one, but everyone has an accent – the way in which you pronounce words. Usually, you will pronounce them in a similar way to people who live in your local area. And, despite the fact that everyone has an accent, we seem to link accents with personality traits, which are sometimes positive and sometimes negative.

Activity 1

a Do you think that having an accent is important in modern Britain?

i Think of well-known people with one of the accents listed below. Here is one to get you started:

Geordie	Ant and Dec
Brummie	
Scottish	
Scouse	
Irish	

ii Now see if you can think of an adjective to describe that person's personality. For example:

Accent	Well-known person	Character
Geordie	Ant and Dec	friendly

b **i** The poll below suggests that people are judged by their accents. Which accent do you think could be perceived to be the most useful in order to get a good job?

ii The Scottish accent is described as 'reassuring'. In what sort of job would it be useful to have a reassuring accent?

What your accent says about you

Various pieces of research have suggested that the way we speak has a huge influence on the way we are perceived.

Geordie

Earlier this year, the Geordie accent was voted the sexiest in Britain. Researchers believe celebrities from Newcastle such as Cheryl Cole have helped raise the profile of the accent, making it seem more friendly and attractive.

Scottish

Scots were found to have the most reassuring accents in Britain, in a recent survey. The Royal National Lifeboat Institution made the discovery in a poll asking which accent people found most soothing in emergencies, although the research did not delve into the numerous regional varieties of the Scottish tongue.

Activity 1 cont.

Scouse

Liverpudlians fared little better in the BBC's research. The accent was said to be viewed by respondents as 'lacking in prestige' and the second most 'unpleasant' to the ear.

Irish

Last year the Irish accent on men was voted the world's sexiest in a poll of 5,000 women. The popularity of stars such as Colin Farrell were said to be the cause of the accent's popularity.

c   What do you think about your accent? What adjectives could be used to describe it?

One profession in particular where accent appears to be important is the legal profession. Read the opening of an article from the periodical *The Lawyer*.

Top firms reject candidates with 'working class accents'

21 December 2010/By Luke McLeod-Roberts

The UK's top law firms are rejecting well-qualified candidates because their accents are too 'working class', according to a new study.

Research carried out by the Cass Business School shows that while elite firms have made strides on increasing recruitment of ethnic minorities into their ranks, working class applicants miss out because they do not fit with the brand.

A partner at one of five case study firms, all of which are in the UK top 20, told Cass Business School: 'There was one guy who came to interviews who was a real Essex barrow boy, and he had a very good CV, he was a clever chap, but we just felt that there's no way we could employ him. I just thought, putting him in front of a client – you just couldn't do it.'

Activity 2

a   This article puts accents into categories. A group of people are 'working class' and another are 'ethnic minorities'. Describe how these different groups' accents might sound.

b   The man who is described as 'a real Essex barrow boy' was not given the job. Explain what the problem with putting an 'Essex barrow boy' in front of a client might be. What is your opinion?

c   Look back at the poll which talks about certain accents lacking prestige. How might accents positively or negatively affect job prospects?

Dialect

Similar to having an accent is speaking a dialect. A dialect is different from an accent because it does not describe how you pronounce words but describes words that you use that are not Standard English. For example:

There are also dialect words used in different parts of the UK. In Norfolk a 'loke' is an alley and in some parts of the country 'nesh'

Standard English

Dialect

'Those girls look cold.'

'Them girls look cold'

means that you feel the cold too easily – for example, some Geordie boys and girls regularly risk freezing to death for fear of being accused of being 'nesh'! Sometimes people's word order shows their dialect.

Some people have the strong view that if you want to get a good job and become successful it is important to speak using Standard English. This does not mean that you do not have an accent but that the words you use are standard and your grammar is too. The article below from the *Daily Mail* is about a school that has decided to make its pupils speak in a certain way so that they are prepared for life after school.

School bans slang! Pupils ordered to use the Queen's English in the classroom 'to help children get jobs'

By Leon Watson

Parents can breathe a sigh of relief – but the local MP isn't impressed.

A school has ordered youngsters to leave slang at the gates and learn to speak the Queen's English.

Sheffield's Springs Academy hopes to give its pupils a better chance of getting a job, so slang or 'text talk' has been banned while they are on the premises.

The United Learning Trust which runs the school, which has 1,100 students aged from 11 to 18 and is in a working-class area of the city, believes slang creates the wrong impression during interviews.

Kathy August, deputy chief executive of the trust, said: 'We want to make sure that our youngsters are not just leaving school with the necessary A to Cs in GCSEs but that they also have a whole range of employability skills.

'We know through the close relationships we have with business partners and commercial partners that when they are doing interviews with youngsters, not only are they looking at the qualifications, they are also looking at how they conduct themselves.

'What we want to make sure of is that they are confident in using standard English. Slang doesn't really give the right impression of the person.

'Youngsters going to interviews for their first job need to make a good impression so that employers have confidence in them.'

Activity 1

a The school's management have decided that the students are going to be banned from using 'slang' or 'text talk'. What sort of words do you think these might be? Look at the table where some slang has been filled in with a suggestion for an acceptable Standard English replacement. Can you think of any more examples?

Slang or text talk	Acceptable version
Lol	That's funny
Hiya	Good morning
Laters	

Activity 1 cont.

b   i   What is the reason given for 'banning' slang and text talk?

      ii   Do you think that this is a good reason?

c   i   Can you think of any jobs or professions in which using text talk or slang:

- would not make any difference.
- would be beneficial.
- would be problematic.

      ii   Are there any jobs where you think it would be acceptable and not make any difference?

Speaking and listening

In pairs, have a go at the following role play that may help you to think about the role of slang and text talk.

One of you should be a sales assistant in an electronics shop who only speaks using slang language. You are helping a customer to choose a laptop and obviously you want them to buy it from your shop.

One of you should be the customer, who only speaks in Standard English.

Act out the conversation – how do the two approaches to spoken language affect the discussion?

Activity 2

Read the following extract which is the second part of the article about Sheffield's Springs Academy and is a criticism of the school's policy.

Ms Smith, a former GCSE English teacher at a South Yorkshire secondary, said: 'The school is wrong to ban slang. How will the school police this?

'Who will say what the difference is between slang and dialect? It could completely undermine the confidence of the children at the school.

'If someone tells them how to speak they could dig in their heels and do it all the more. I really think they have set themselves a task that is impossible to achieve.'

Ms Smith said: 'Who is going to adjudicate? Who is going to say slang, dialect or accent? And which one is right and which one is wrong?

'Most people know when to put on their telephone voice because that is what we are talking about. When people go on the phone or talk to anyone in authority they put on a different voice.'

a   Ms Smith disagrees with the school's policy. Write a list of bullet points showing the reasons that she uses to argue against it. The first is done for you:

- It is very difficult to check up on. Teachers cannot listen to pupils all of the time to check on what words they are using.

b   Ms Smith uses the phrase 'telephone voice' and talks about having a 'different voice'. Do you think that this is true of yourself? Can you think of different times when you have a 'telephone' voice?

c   Write a letter to the *Daily Mail* newspaper explaining your views, pointing out what you see as the advantages and potential pitfalls of the school's policy.

It's like just bare wrong, innit?

Another area of language use that leads to quite strong views is that of the way young people talk compared to those who are older. This is not just a recent issue; people have complained for centuries about the changes that young people make to language and how they use language. While you might be tempted to just turn around and say 'Allow it, bruv', 40 years ago you would probably have said something like 'Hey, don't bum me out with your square talk, man'.

In recent years, with the growth of texting and instant messaging, there have been even more complaints about how young people use language. Have a look at the extract that follows and see what you make of the different views being put forward.

That Emma Thompson's, like, well annoyed, innit

The Oxford-educated actress has hit out at slang used by the young, claiming it makes them sound stupid when they're not. The 51-year-old, known for her roles in Shakespeare film adaptations, said the use of sloppy language made her feel 'insane'.

'I went to give a talk at my old school and the girls were all doing their "likes" and "innits?" and "it ain'ts", which drives me insane,' she told the *Radio Times*.

'I told them "Just don't do it. Because it makes you sound stupid and you're not stupid." There is the necessity to have two languages – one that you use with your mates and the other that you need in any official capacity.'

Activity 3

a
 i   Do you agree with Emma Thompson's points in the first extract?
 ii Do you have any particular words that you really do not like to hear?

b Read the following. Which points do you think support Emma Thompson's views and which do not?

 A Slang gives the impression that younger people don't understand how to use language properly when that's far from the case.

 B Of course there's a place for modern slang. Language, by nature, is dynamic and it shouldn't always be formal.

 C Language is a melting pot and there are loads of influences on it. But bad influences are contributing to making English teaching difficult.

 D The danger of young people using language like that is that people assume they're somehow stupid. And that isn't true.

 E Language is always evolving. 'Proper' English approved by the Oxford dictionary – as opposed to slang or colloquialisms – would still eventually evolve because the way we use words always changes.

 F There are so many more influences, such as American TV shows and the net, on children that make our jobs as English teachers much more difficult.

 G Yesterday's slang is today's Standard English – some slang words become accepted into formal English and others die out.

 H In certain situations, Standard English is not as expressive as slang; it's not as emotional.

c Is the use of slang, popularised by hip-hop artists and television shows, really such a bad thing? Give reasons and examples to support your point of view.

Glossary

Adjective: a word used to describe a person, place or thing.

Ad-lib: to make something up on the spot or to say something unprepared.

Back-channelling: the supportive words or sounds that are used to indicate that we are listening and interested in a conversation.

Cohesion: the way that a text or piece of speech holds together through features such as repeated words and structures.

Colloquial: describes language that is chatty and informal but which everyone can understand.

Command: an utterance where one speaker tells another to carry out an action.

Compressed grammar: text that is reduced to some of its most important parts and leaves out bits that can be worked out from the context.

Computer-mediated communication (CMC): a means of communicating that uses some kind of electronic device such as a mobile phone, PC or laptop. It is neither written nor spoken but usually typed on a keypad.

Confirmation checks: words and phrases used to check if the listener is following.

Conjunctions: words used to link together other words, phrases or clauses (e.g. 'and', 'but', 'if').

Connotations: the ideas or feelings associated with a particular word.

Context: the situation in which spoken language is used. It includes factors such as who is interacting, what their relationship is, their purpose, where they are, who is listening, what else is going on around them, and so on.

Context dependent: relying on the immediate environment to make complete sense.

Cue: language that acts as a prompt.

Denotation: the literal, dictionary meaning of a word. This is often different to the connotations the word may have.

Direct: to be explicit in putting forward your thoughts.

Directive: a sentence or utterance acting as a kind of command or order.

Discourse markers: words or expressions that draw listeners' attention to what is coming next.

Dynamic verbs: verbs that describe physical actions.

Ellipsis: missing out words, phrases or larger clause elements.

Emoticon: a symbol used in CMC to express emotion or attitude.

Emotive: describes a word or phrase that provokes a strong emotional response in the audience.

Explicit meaning: the meaning is very clear and there is no room for interpretation. The opposite of implied meaning.

False start: where you start, stop, and then start again in what you say. This often happens at the beginning of an utterance but it can also happen halfway through.

Filler: a word or phrase that does not appear to add much meaning but which might allow the speaker a bit of extra time to think about what they really want to say.

Formal: describes language that is polite, official or complex.

Hyperbole: an exaggerated statement.

Imperative: a sentence that acts as a command.

Informal: describes language that is casual, friendly or unofficial.

Interactional: when the social relationships are more important than the message.

Interrogative: a sentence that acts as a question.

Intonation: the way in which pitch goes up and down in speech.

Jargon: special words or phrases including subject-specific words that are used by a particular profession or group.

Latching on (=): describes conversations where there is no gap between the participant's utterances. A bracket with a dot in the middle (.) is a short pause.

Lexis: a technical term for words or vocabulary.

Metaphor: a word or expression that suggests a comparison with something else but which is not meant literally.

Modal verb: a type of verb that works with a main verb to add a degree of certainty, obligation or doubt.

Oratory: public speaking; skill in public speaking.

Overlapping: talking at the same time as someone else. This can be marked in a number of ways. In this book we have indicated this by placing // at the beginning and end of the overlap.

Phatic communication: a type of warming up; you are getting yourself ready for the demands of the person that you are talking to and the context of the talk.

Primary purpose: the main aim of what you are trying to communicate.

Quotative: an expression used to describe the way in which someone said something.

Register: the style of language used in a particular context; language can have a formal, informal or mixed register.

Repair: changing the wording of what you were originally going to say.

Rhetoric: the art of using language persuasively and effectively.

Scheme: a generally or expected agreed structure to a familiar type of interaction.

Secondary purpose: other aims you might have.

Signposting device: a word or phrase used to help listeners follow the structure of what is being said.

Slang: very informal words and phrases that are used and understood by only certain groups of people.

Spontaneous speech: speech that is not planned or rehearsed.

Standard English: this is the variety of English that is agreed to be grammatically correct and uses vocabulary that is understood by most English speakers, regardless of region.

Statements (declaratives): utterances or clauses that state a point (rather than asking a question or giving a command).

Subject-specific: any words that are closely connected to a specialist subject.

Subtext: similar to an implied meaning and describes the concept that what we say is not necessarily what we mean.

Tone: refers to the emotions behind a speaker's utterance. Tone is created by the sound of your voice, by the pitch, pace and speed that you talk at, and even by the words you choose.

Transactional: when language has a message as its main focus.

Transcript: words written down exactly as they have been spoken.

Turn-taking: the normal structure of conversations in which one speaker's turn (what they have to say) is followed by another's.

Utterance: when someone speaks, we usually refer to each unit of speech as an utterance. This term can be used for very tiny or very long amounts of speech that are said all in one go.

Vague language: expressions typical in speech which are often used to finish utterances or to make the speaker sound less certain.

Voiced pause: a pause in which the speaker makes a sound, for example 'erm'.

Acknowledgements

The author and the publisher would also like to thank the following for permission to reproduce material:

Text permissions pages 4 and 19, extracts from *The Only Way is Essex*, produced by Lime Pictures; pp16–17, Radio interview with Tulisa *Young*, reproduced with permission of KissFM UK; p24, Radio phone-in, talkSPORT; pp29–31, extracts from *Oleanna* by David Mamet; p35, Excerpt from KES adapted by Lawrence Till from Barry Hines' *A Kestrel for a Knave* copyright © 2000 Barry Hines and Lawrence Till. Reprinted by arrangement with the publisher: www.nickhernbooks.co.uk; p39, *Our Day Out* by Willy Russell, sourced from *Studio Scripts – Our Day Out and Other Plays* first published by Nelson Thornes in 1991, last reprint 2010; pp40–1, Screenplay *The Wild One* by John Paxton and Ben Maddow, first released 1953; p50, text reproduced courtesy of QMU; pp59–60, Michelle Obama to the Democratic Party Convention in September 2012; pp61–2, transcript of Bill Clinton's Speech to the Democratic National Convention; p70, *Pigeon English* by Stephan Kelman, published by Bloomsbury, 2011; pp70–1, extract from Friday Night Dinner, Big Talk Productions Ltd; pp72–3, extract from *The Inbetweeners* by Damon Beesley and Iain Morris, Bwark Productions; p76, *Educating Essex*, Channel 4, Twofour Productions; p77, Channel 4 News interview; pp78–9, extract from *The Family, Series 1*, Channel 4; pp81–3, Excerpts from *Death of Salesman* by Arthur Miller. Copyright © 1949, Arthur Miller, used by permission of The Wylie Agency (UK) Limited; p87, extract from The Lawyer, 21 December 2010; p88, © *Daily Mail*, 'Schools ban slang! Pupils ordered to use the Queen's English in the classroom "to help children get jobs"' by Leon Watson, 15 February 2012; p90, 'That Emma Thompson's like, well annoyed, innit' reproduced courtesy of *Mirrorpix*.

Every effort had been made to trace the copyright holders but if any have been inadvertently overlooked the publisher will be pleased to make the necessary arrangements at the first opportunity.